HISTORY IN DEPTH

THE GREAT WAR

Vincent Crinnion

Head of History, Leftwich High School, Northwich

M
MACMILLAN
EDUCATION

For Katy

First published 1986
Reprinted 1987, 1988

Published by
MACMILLAN EDUCATION LTD
Houndmills, Basingstoke, Hampshire RG21 2XS
and London
Companies and representatives
throughout the world

Printed in Hong Kong

British Library Cataloguing in Publication Data
Crinnion, Vincent
The Great War.—(History in depth).
1. World War, 1914-1918
I. Title II. Series
940.3   D522.7
ISBN 0-333-38589-6

CONTENTS

Preface   4

1   A death in Sarajevo   5

2   The time bomb   8

3   From Schlieffen to stalemate   19

4   The new warfare   25

5   Deadlock, 1915–17   35

6   Different dimensions   43

7   Nations at war   53

8   The final acts   59

Index   64

Acknowledgements

The author and publishers wish to thank the following who has kindly given permission for the use of copyright material:

George T. Sassoon for *Glory of Women* by Seigfried Sassoon, p 56.

The author and publishers wish to acknowledge, with thanks, the following photograph sources:

BBC Hulton Picture Library pp 14 left, 47; Bilderdienst Suddeutscher Verlag p 36; The *Daily Mirror* p 55 bottom; The Imperial War Museum pp 25, 27, 28, 29, 30, 32, 39, 44, 57, 58; Macdonald Publishers p 11; Popperfoto p 7.

The publishers have made every effort to trace the copyright holders, but if they have inadvertently overlooked any, they will be pleased to make the necessary arrangements at the first opportunity.

PREFACE

The study of history is exciting, whether in a good story well told, a mystery solved by the judicious unravelling of clues, or a study of the men, women and children whose fears and ambitions, successes and tragedies make up the collective memory of mankind.

This series aims to reveal this excitement to pupils through a set of topic books on important historical subjects from the Middle Ages to the present day. Each book contains four main elements: a narrative and descriptive text, lively and relevant illustrations, extracts of contemporary evidence, and questions for further thought and work. Involvement in these elements should provide an adventure which will bring the past to life in the imagination of the pupil.

Each book is also designed to develop the knowledge, skills and concepts so essential to a pupil's growth. It provides a wide, varying introduction to the evidence available on each topic. In handling this evidence, pupils will increase their understanding of basic historical concepts such as causation and change, as well as of more advanced ideas such as revolution and democracy. In addition, their use of basic study skills will be complemented by more sophisticated historical skills such as the detection of bias and the formulation of opinion.

The intended audience for the series is pupils of eleven to sixteen years: it is expected that the earlier topics will be introduced in the first three years of secondary school, while the nineteenth and twentieth century topics are directed towards first examinations.

A DEATH IN SARAJEVO

. . . I do not let myself be kept under a glass cover. Our life is constantly in danger. One has to rely on God.

Archduke Franz Ferdinand, 1914

The year was 1914. Europe sweltered in a heatwave that had lasted for weeks. In a small hillside town called Sarajevo, the population busily prepared itself for a state occasion. Archduke Franz Ferdinand, heir to the throne of the Austro-Hungarian Empire, was visiting the city with his wife, Countess Sophie. They were there chiefly to inspect the Austrian army but also to celebrate their wedding anniversary.

From the beginning of their visit the royal couple were cheered everywhere they went. Security was very lax; there were no soldiers and very few police. Brightly coloured flags hung out of top windows and the sunlit streets were lined with admiring citizens.

Sunday, 28 June. The Archduke was dressed in a blue tunic and black trousers. His wife wore a white silk dress. They rode in a procession of four cars and as they passed along the route to the town hall they waved at the crowd, who gave them a friendly reception.

At various places along the route six men looked around them and waited nervously. They had come to Sarajevo to celebrate a different occasion from the rest of the crowd – the assassination of Archduke Franz Ferdinand. They were members of a secret terrorist organisation called the Black Hand, which wanted to make all Slav people free from the Austrian Empire. The Black Hand also wanted more power inside the government of Serbia (see map on page 17). The organisation was willing to kill to gain its ends.

10.10 a.m. A tall man in a long black coat and a hat asked a policeman which car the Archduke was in. The second car, he was told. As the cars moved past, this same man pulled a hand grenade from his pocket, knocked the cap off it against a lamp post and hurled it at the Archduke's car. The driver saw the bomb fly towards him and accelerated his car; the bomb bounced away underneath the next car in the procession. The explosion caused panic and injury but missed its royal target. About 20 people lay on the pavements wounded. Others screamed hysterically and panicking policemen arrested onlookers indiscriminately. The damaged car was pushed on to the pavement and the Archduke shouted: 'The fellow must be insane. Gentlemen, let us proceed with our programme.'

Unknown to the Archduke other desperate men awaited their chance. One man could not get the bomb out of his pocket because of the crowds jammed against his side.

While all this was happening Gavrilo Princip, a 19-year-old Serb, was wondering what to do. He was a member of the Black Hand and at first he thought that their plot had succeeded. Then to his horror he saw the Archduke go past, very much alive. Depressed and confused he crossed the road to a café, ordered a cup of coffee and sat down. In his pocket was a revolver. He had fired a few practice shots during the previous few days, but had missed the target. Besides, they had been taught to fire on stationary objects, not moving cars!

10.45 a.m. The Archduke was angry. His anniversary had been spoilt and Sophie had a graze on her neck. He cut short the reception at the town hall, decided to visit a policeman injured in the bomb attack and changed the pre-arranged route accordingly. The cars roared along the quay at high speed until they came to Franz Joseph Street. For some reason the driver of the first car, followed by the second, turned right – along the original route. 'What is this? Stop!' shouted an official in the Archduke's car. 'You are going the wrong way.' Brakes were jammed on, an engine stalled and one driver struggled noisily to find reverse gear in his car.

Princip could not believe his luck. (Afterwards some people said the driver's mistake was deliberate.) He pushed through the crowd with his revolver. A policeman saw what was happening and tried to grab Princip but was hit by someone behind him. Princip jumped on to the car's running board and fired at point-blank range. The royal couple slumped forward. The Archduke cried out: 'Sophie, Sophie don't die. Live for my children.' Within minutes they were both dead.

11.30 a.m. Church bells rang solemnly, one after another, through-out the city. Some of the assassins, including Princip, were arrested. They tried to swallow poison that they had been given by their leaders in case things went wrong. The poison did not work. Princip later died of disease and ill-treatment in prison.

Using the evidence: who was to blame?
The death of the Archduke caused great controversy. Various people and factors were blamed for the killing. Use the evidence provided to decide which of the possible theories (listed below) is the most acceptable. Try to find facts in each piece of evidence that (a) support (b) disprove each theory.

Theories		Facts (to be discovered in the evidence)
1 Bad planning by the authorities	Yes/No	
2 Chance (i.e. luck or fate)	Yes/No	
3 Well-planned plot by trained killers	Yes/No	
4 Accident (i.e. killed the wrong man)	Yes/No	

A A modern diagram of the fateful route taken on 28 June 1914

A The unsuccessful bomb attack took place here

B The site of the successful shooting

5 Princip's first position

6 Princip's second position

1–4, 7 The position of the other assassins

Franz Ferdinand's route to town hall

The original return route from town hall

The changed return route, after bombing

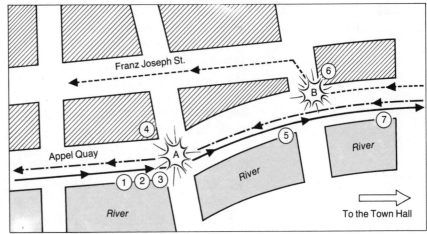

B A contemporary photograph of the incident: Archduke Franz Ferdinand and Sophie leave the town hall

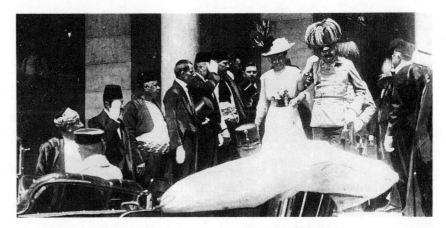

C Gavrilo Princip's own statement:

When the second car arrived, I recognised the heir-apparent. But as I saw that a lady was sitting next to him I reflected for a moment whether I should shoot or not. At the same moment I was filled with a peculiar feeling and I aimed at the heir-apparent from the pavement . . . where I aimed I do not know. But I know that I aimed at the heir-apparent. I believe that I fired twice, perhaps more, because I was so excited. Whether I hit the victim or not, I cannot tell, because instantly people started to hit me.
Quoted in J. Hamer's book, *The Twentieth Century*, 1980

D A secondary account of what happened (pages 5–6)

THE TIME BOMB

> *If I hadn't done it, the Germans would have found some other excuse.*
>
> Gavrilo Princip, 1914

Wars break out when one country attacks another. But what causes a whole continent to go to war? Why did a single assassination in a remote Balkan state provoke the seven most powerful countries in the world (and more than 20 other nations) to eventually declare war? For this is what happened. Within only five weeks of the death of Archduke Franz Ferdinand, the Great War had begun.

There is no simple answer to explain what caused the Great War. By 1914 Europe had become like a time bomb with a short fuse. This explosive situation was made up of many different factors, some of which originated in the nineteenth century.

An empire for Germany

By 1900 the Great Powers of Europe controlled most of the known world. Some countries, such as Britain and France, had gradually built up their empires since the seventeenth century. (An empire is a group of overseas territories, called colonies, that are controlled by another country. Belief in this system is known as colonialism or imperialism.)

From 1889 Wilhelm II, Germany's new monarch, set out to make his nation into a first-rate world power. He was intensely jealous of Britain's enormous empire. The modern state of Germany had only

Major European colonies in 1914

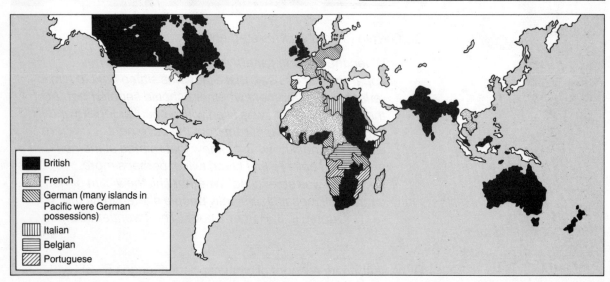

British

French

German (many islands in Pacific were German possessions)

Italian

Belgian

Portuguese

been in existence since 1871 and had been left well behind in the European race for overseas colonies.

Germany had quickly become a hard-working, prosperous and orderly nation. By 1900 its economy was even rivalling Britain's, especially in the manufacture of cars, chemicals and steel. A large overseas empire would help the German economy even more.

Despite Wilhelm II's ambitions, there was little of value left in the world for Germany to conquer. His self-confidence and aggression made the other Great Powers nervous. Their empires were precious and might need protection.

Colonial clashes: from Berlin to Bosnia
This rivalry over colonies was a major cause of international tension between the Great Powers.

Date	Issue	Outcome
1898	British control of Sudan and Upper Nile.	War narrowly avoided between Britain and France.
1890s	German control of parts of Africa and New Guinea.	Constant tension between Britain and Germany.
	German railway from Berlin to Baghdad threatened British and Russian interests in the Middle East.	International tension between Great Powers.
1905	Morocco's independence used by Germany to test Anglo-French alliance.	Germany overruled by Britain and France at Algeciras Conference (1906).
1911	" "	Germany forced to back down after sending gunboat, *Panther*, to port of Agadir.
1905	Control of Korea.	Captured by Japan after a war against Russia.
1908	Austrian invasion of Bosnia, a Turkish province.	War narrowly avoided against Russia, which backed down.

These various crises had long-term consequences. They created anger and resentment which lingered long after the actual incidents. Germany became convinced that it was being encircled by its enemies and therefore enlarged its armed forces. Britain, France and Russia became closer allies because of German aggression. Russia looked for revenge on Austria after the Bosnian humiliation (see page 16).

The crises also showed that declaring war on one country often meant war with other countries as well. Why?

Two hostile camps: the alliance system

Between 1882 and 1907 Europe's Great Powers had created a complicated web of diplomatic alliances. The two most important of these were the so-called Entente Cordiale (Britain, France and Russia), and the Triple Alliance (Germany, Austria and Italy). In effect, they divided Europe into two hostile camps.

Each individual alliance was different from the others in terms of what was agreed, but two dominant threads can be traced:

1. Germany felt secure only as long as France was isolated and as long as Germany did not become *encircled* by hostile powers.
2. Britain preferred to remain in 'splendid isolation' from European affairs unless she felt that her colonial interests were *threatened* by other nations, especially Germany. From 1900 onwards Britain's anxieties over this question quickly increased.

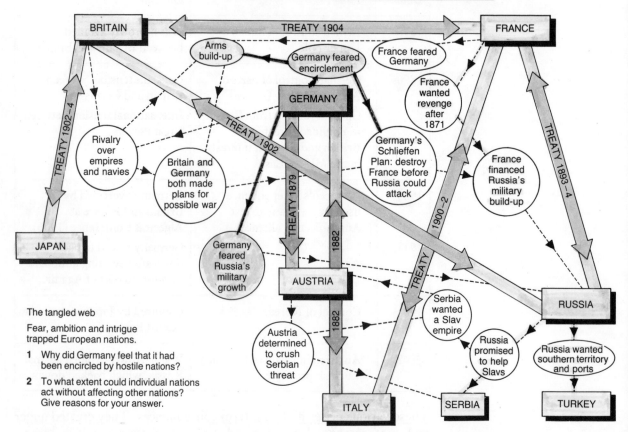

The tangled web

Fear, ambition and intrigue trapped European nations.

1. Why did Germany feel that it had been encircled by hostile nations?
2. To what extent could individual nations act without affecting other nations? Give reasons for your answer.

Using the evidence: the shifting scene

Since 1879 Germany and other countries had tried to strengthen their own positions by making agreements with other nations about territories, trade and war. However, each new agreement between countries could later produce yet another treaty signed by their rivals.

European alliances and treaties in 1914

1. Study the cartoon above. What seems to be the main purpose of these alliances?

2. Now compare the cartoon with the information about treaties on the diagram on page 10. What has happened to Europe's alliances?

3. Now also consider the map of Europe in 1914 on page 17. How far have the following British and German priorities been maintained:
   a) France to be isolated?
   b) Germany not to be encircled?
   c) Britain not to become involved?
   Refer to the diagrams and give reasons for your answers.

4. Copy the table below and use all the available information to complete it.

Date of major alliance	Britain: and its allies?	Germany: and its allies?	France: and its allies?
? 1882 1887	None	Austria	None
?		Austria, Italy	Russia
1902 1907	France, Japan France, Japan Russia		

The arms race

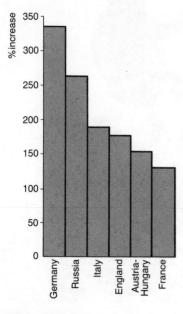

Spending on armaments, 1872–1912

Europe had prepared for war long before 1914. Whatever its size each major power made sure that its military strength was as great as the country could afford. Between 1870 and 1914 military spending by the European powers increased by 300 per cent. After 1871 all the major nations (except Britain) brought in conscription, which meant that men were forced to serve a minimum period in the armed services. Germany on its own could put 5 600 000 trained soldiers into battle if war broke out. Two international conferences were held in 1899 and 1907 to limit the arms race, but both ended in failure.

There were two main reasons for this acceleration in military expenditure. Firstly, it was thought to be the only way to keep the peace. After all, argued the generals and admirals among others, no enemy would attack a well-defended country. Popular newspapers helped to spread this attitude. In 1909 the *Daily Mail* provocatively reported:

> *Germany is deliberately preparing to destroy the British Empire. . . .*
> *We are all to be drilled and schooled and uniformed by [German]*
> *officials. . . . Britain alone stands in the way of Germany's [path to]*
> *world power and domination.*

A second reason for the arms race concerned the overseas colonies. Germany believed that it would never be able to enlarge its empire until it had a powerful navy like Britain's. Therefore, at the end of the nineteenth century, Germany began to build a fleet of warships that would rival any in the world. This made Britain feel that its security, at home and abroad, was under threat from Germany. In 1906 it was Germany's turn to be worried. Britain launched a powerful new battleship called HMS *Dreadnought*, which was faster and more powerful than any other battleship afloat.

The Germans quickly decided to build their own *Dreadnought*-style ship, and the Kiel Canal in Germany was widened to take the ships' extra width. Britain was alarmed. Soon both countries were involved in a race to build the most battleships and battlecruisers.

	Number of battleships and battlecruisers	
	Germany	Britain
1906	0	1
1909	3	3
1913	5	8
Total by 1914	24	38

War dreams

Before 1914 people from all social classes accepted that war was a natural and honourable way of settling international disputes. In 1899 a German historian wrote:

> We want to be a World Power.... Here there can be no step backward.... We can pursue this policy with England or without England. With England means in peace; against England means – through war.
>
> Quoted in H. Mills' book, *The Road to Sarajevo*, 1983

Ordinary people grew up to accept this general attitude. At school children were taught the virtues of their own country and the sins of neighbouring nations. Popular daily newspapers exploited and sensationalised military items. Often they reacted to the actions of foreign countries in a hysterical and prejudiced manner. Many war novels became best sellers.

One British book, *Invasion of 1910*, sold over a million copies after being serialised in the *Daily Mail*. Between 1900 and 1914 more than 180 books about imaginary future wars were published throughout Europe! And it was Germany that was now identified as Britain's main enemy in many of these books. Before 1900 the traditional enemy was usually France.

It is little wonder then that the outbreak of real fighting in 1914 was greeted with the greatest popular support in the history of warfare.

War plans

Long before 1914 all the major European powers had prepared complicated military plans to ensure victory. These plans were all based on the nineteenth-century idea that to be successful an army had to strike quickly and decisively with huge numbers of soldiers. It was widely believed that the first strike might easily be the last strike. If this was true, the generals argued, then it followed that an army should *attack first* in order to *defend* itself!

The most important of all these military schemes was the Schlieffen Plan. It was devised in secrecy by the Chief of the German General Staff, Alfred von Schlieffen. By 1905 he had calculated how the German army could defeat France and Russia on two different fighting fronts without having to divide his army. Firstly, a massive assault at lightning speed was to be launched against the French, who were expected to surrender within six weeks. The German army was then to be switched by railway to eastern Europe before the Russian army had time to assemble equipment and supplies and to move its soldiers into position (this is known as mobilisation).

Schlieffen's scheme was a masterpiece of planning. Most of its details were correct <u>but several basic ideas behind the plan proved to be wrong</u>. These were:

1 *That any future war <u>would</u> involve France*. Schlieffen did not allow for a war with Russia only. Therefore when Russia mobilised its armies in 1914 Germany was still obliged by the Schlieffen Plan to attack France first.

2 *That France would be defeated before the German army attacked Russia*. As it turned out, however, Germany had to fight Russia and France at the same time.

3 *That Britain would not get involved in the fighting*. Schlieffen did not take account of the fact that Belgium was neutral (which meant that it was free from ties with other countries and safe from attack or invasion), and that Britain had promised to protect its neutrality as long ago as 1839. For the sake of speed, Schlieffen ordered a huge number of trains carrying soldiers, equipment, supplies and horses to cross the Belgian frontier immediately. By then, of course, Belgian neutrality had been broken – the war had started.

<u>Perhaps the biggest weakness in Schlieffen's plan was that it was far too rigid</u>. Once the German war machine had been set in motion it was virtually impossible to stop it. Railway timetables would take months to rewrite. Worse still, it would signal to an enemy that Germany had started to attack, then had changed its mind and was now defenceless. <u>For Germany, therefore, mobilisation meant all-out war. The Schlieffen Plan left virtually no time for negotiations and peace proposals.</u>

Using the evidence: the warmonger

The Allies (Britain, France and Russia) always blamed Germany for causing the war. In a sense, of course, Germany did provoke conflict initially by invading Belgium. Some historians now think that Germany not only caused the war but wanted war and planned for it. At the centre of this activity was the Kaiser, Wilhelm II. He had a reputation for stirring up trouble and was said to be a warmonger. Was this true?

A (left) *An official photograph of Wilhelm II in full military uniform*

B (right) *A British postcard of 1914*

HE WON'T BE HAPPY TILL HE GETS IT

EUROPE

C *Give no quarter! Take no prisoners! Anybody who falls into your hands must be destroyed. Just as a thousand years ago Attila's Huns made a reputation for ruthless violence that still resounds through the ages, so let the name of Germans, through your actions in China, acquire a similar reputation that will last for a thousand years . . . .*

Wilhelm II, in a speech to his troops, 1900

partisan: supporter

D *I was always a partisan of peace; but this has its limits. I have read much about war and know what it means. But finally a situation arises in which a great power can no longer just look on, but must draw the sword!*

Wilhelm II, October 1913

1 What impression was source A meant to give of the Kaiser? Refer to details in the photograph to explain your answer.

2 Read sources C and D. They both provide clues about the Kaiser's attitude to war.
   a) In what way do they agree?
   b) In what way does source C contradict the Kaiser's claim that 'I was always a partisan of peace'?

3 Historians need to know if the information in their sources is reliable. Sources A and B are both examples of propaganda.
   a) Explain why each of these might not provide totally accurate views of the attitude of the Kaiser.
   b) Explain how these sources could still be very useful to the historian.

4 'The Kaiser was a warmonger and caused the Great War.' Consider each of the sources.
   a) Use them as evidence to write a paragraph which supports this statement.
   b) Why does your answer to (a) give an unbalanced view of the Kaiser's attitude?
   c) Find other evidence in this chapter to contradict the statement above.

Nationalism

One of the most basic causes of the war was the extreme loyalty people felt towards their own country. This nationalism was a very powerful force; it bewitched all kinds of people in many parts of Europe. France resented that Germany had captured Alsace-Lorraine in 1870–71. Germany resented British influence in Africa. The Balkan states of south-eastern Europe became known as the 'powder keg' because nationalistic feelings ran so high; several states wanted freedom from their Austrian and Ottoman rulers.

To complicate matters even more, Russia saw herself as a champion of the Slavs in the Balkan peninsular. Russia promised them support. Other European powers, including Britain, France and Germany, watched the area nervously. They were indirectly involved because of their alliances with Russia and Austria. After 1908 their unease over the Balkan 'powder keg' increased. A series of international incidents sent the sparks flying.

Balkan incident	Details	Main consequences
The Bosnian Crisis, 1908	A revolution in Turkey allowed Austria to seize control of Bosnia. Serbia protested to Russia. Germany supported Austria. Russia backed down.	1 Russia angrily began to build up its armed forces and looked for revenge. 2 Serbia began to support anti-Austrian groups, such as the Black Hand terrorists.
First Balkan War, 1912	Newly-formed Balkan League (Serbia, Greece, Bulgaria, Montenegro) attacked Turkey and drove her out of all European territories. Austria called for war against Serbia. European powers forced a peaceful settlement. Balkan League shared Turkish lands.	1 Serbia became the most powerful Balkan state. She now dreamt of controlling a Slav empire in the Balkans. 2 Austria was determined to crush Serbia before her own empire was threatened. 3 The European alliance system was put under great strain. Russia and Germany became open enemies.
Second Balkan War, 1913	Quarrelling inside Balkan League led to war between Bulgaria and the rest. Bulgaria was quickly defeated and lost new territories.	
The Sarajevo Assassination, 1914	A young Serb killed the heir to the Austrian throne in Bosnia.	1 Austrian threats to Serbia forced Russia to mobilise to support the Serbs. 2 Germany mobilised to help Austria and attacked France. 3 Britain was drawn into war.

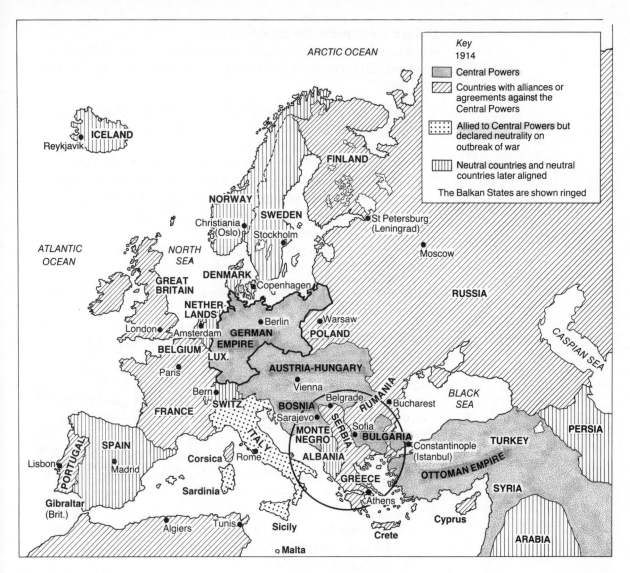

Europe in 1914

The following appears in the map legend:

Key
1914

- Central Powers
- Countries with alliances or agreements against the Central Powers
- Allied to Central Powers but declared neutrality on outbreak of war
- Neutral countries and neutral countries later aligned

The Balkan States are shown ringed

A spark for the fuse

The Sarajevo assassination on 28 June 1914 provided the spark which ignited the time bomb that Europe had become. Europe had survived many crises in the past but Sarajevo seemed to provide one crisis too many. What had kept Europe at peace – alliances, strong armed forces and colonial distractions – now helped to send Europe to war. Few people were disappointed by the outbreak of war and even fewer were surprised by it.

In 1914 the generals and politicians in Germany had looked on war as essential if they were to survive as a world power. It was to be a quick war; everybody said it would be over by Christmas; but it was to last for four years. In August 1914, six million soldiers moved into combat. By November 1918 more than 65 million men had put on uniform. A war to end all wars, they said in 1918 – the Great War.

Using the evidence: the causes of war

Historians like to explain why things happen. It is very difficult, however, to be certain about the cause of certain events, such as wars. Why?

1 Often there are many causes. Which ones, therefore, are the most important? Do they interact with one another? Can important events occur by accident?
2 The beginnings of events can often be traced back many years. Could events such as the Great War therefore have occurred at an earlier time? Do certain factors have to be present to trigger off an event? If so, what were the factors that triggered off the war in 1914?
3 People do not always explain why they act in a particular way. What outside factors affect people's decisions?

Use these points and what you have read in chapters 1 and 2 to complete the exercises below.

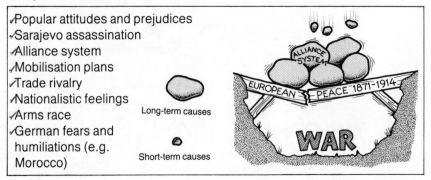

- ✓Popular attitudes and prejudices
- ✓Sarajevo assassination
- ✓Alliance system
- ✓Mobilisation plans
- ✓Trade rivalry
- ✓Nationalistic feelings
- ✓Arms race
- ✓German fears and humiliations (e.g. Morocco)

Long-term causes

Short-term causes

a) The causes
   (i) Decide which of the causes in the list are long term and which are short term. Copy out and complete the diagram.
   (ii) Justify your choices.
   (iii) Can you think of another way of presenting this information in picture form?

b) The blame
   Who was most responsible for the outbreak of war?

Culprit	Ranking 1–7	Reasons for ranking
Gavrilo Princip Austria Germany Arms manufacturers Russia Britain Ordinary people		

3 FROM SCHLIEFFEN TO STALEMATE

In the West the armies were too big for the country; in the East the country was too big for the armies.

Winston Churchill

On 4 August 1914, the German army(one and a half million strong) swept across the Belgian frontier on its way to France. This was the beginning of a long and bloody war.

Schlieffen's Plan was a gamble that never came off. For one thing it relied on speed of attack, but the German army's early progress of 48 kilometres a day soon slowed down. Also, Belgian soldiers fiercely resisted the massive German war machine. The fortress of Liège held out for 12 days until heavy artillery, so large it had to be mounted on railway waggons, smashed the defences into pieces. However, when Brussels fell the Belgian resistance collapsed and the German army marched quickly into France.

Again the Germans met fierce opposition, this time from the newly arrived British Expeditionary Force (BEF) led by Sir John French. This small British army had been sent to provide the Belgians and French with support on their left wing. To their horror the Old Contemptibles found themselves unexpectedly in the middle of the main German advance. Nevertheless, they surprised the Germans with their courage and the speed and accuracy of their rifle fire. Indeed, the Germans thought they were being fired on by machine guns! On 23 August vicious fighting took place among the pit-heads and slag heaps of Mons. By the time the BEF had been forced back, the French, who had been badly shaken by early clashes, were able to regroup their forces. In addition, the Russian army had mobilised far quicker than expected. They were now poised menacingly on Germany's eastern front. By now Schlieffen's timetable for total victory had been badly upset.

At the end of August German troops were only 80 kilometres from Paris and could see the Eiffel Tower through binoculars. The French government quickly moved out of the city to safety in Bordeaux. By now, however, another fatal error in Schlieffen's plan had become obvious. The front line troops, who were exhausted and footsore, had lost contact with the main German headquarters. Food supplies could not get through because the narrow country roads were blocked with hundreds of thousands of soldiers, horses and pieces of equipment. Some columns stretched back 128 kilometres!

Old Contemptibles: a nickname for the BEF, based on a remark supposedly made by Wilhelm II: 'A contemptible little army.'

The war of movement

By 5 September the German army was faced with the combined force of the Allies. Nearly 600 taxis were used to rush 6000 French reinforcements to the front line near the River Marne. The occasion marked the first use of mechanised road transport in warfare.

The battle of the Marne lasted two weeks and stretched along a 240-kilometre front – it was a crucial battle of manoeuvre rather than great fighting. At one point a gap opened up in the German line, but Sir John French thought it might be a trap and hesitated. General Joffre, the French Commander-in-Chief, was bolder. He launched a massive counter-attack and cut the German front line in two. The Germans desperately tried to plug the gap but failed. After five days of confused fighting they retreated to a new line at the River Aisne. Both sides dug shallow trenches and waited.

This defeat was greeted with horror by Helmuth von Moltke, the German Commander-in-Chief. By now he was a broken man, depressed and exhausted. The Allies were closer to victory than at any other time before 1918. The Germans had lost the chance of a quick victory in the west and the rest of the war would have to be fought on two fronts after all.

The Germans and British both raced their armies north to capture the vital ports of Dunkirk, Calais and Boulogne. Each army tried unsuccessfully to get behind the other. Antwerp fell to the Germans but the Belgians stopped any further advance by flooding the land around Nieuport.

A vicious battle now began near Ypres, the only major Belgian town left in Allied hands. It was the first of many bloody struggles around

The western front: 700 kms of trenches containing 4 million troops

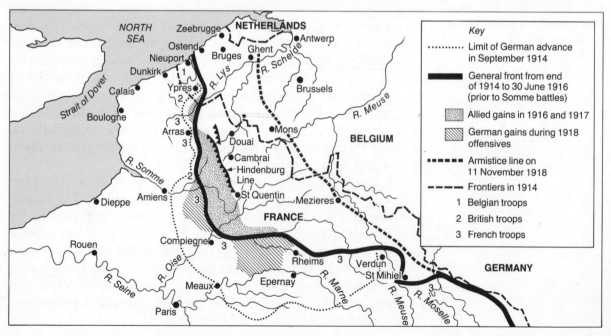

the place that the British troops called 'Wipers'. The months of October and November gave both sides a bitter taste of things to come. The fighting was bloody and merciless. Soldiers fought hand-to-hand in the woods around Ypres and in the end 50 000 Britons were lost in order to hold a town that had no strategic value.

The autumn clashes had produced horrifying numbers of casualties for all the armies.

	Size of army	Casualties
Britain	160 000	85 000
France	1 000 000	850 000
Germany	1 500 000	677 000

In December, Moltke was replaced by a younger and more positive man, Erich von Falkenhayn, who decided to switch the German forces to the Channel coast in order to cut off British supplies and to prevent more troops from arriving there.

The clash in the east

On the eastern front Germany and the armies of the Austrian Empire confronted Russia and Serbia.

A different kind of war developed on this front. Here, highly mobile, massive armies, clashed in savage battles. The fighting front was 1450 kilometres long and it was relatively easy for armies to outmanoeuvre, outmarch or outflank their opponents. Even more important were the vast distances *behind* the front fighting lines, which caused great problems with communications, supplies and reinforcements. The Germans were eventually to win the war in the east in 1917, mainly because they were able to overcome these problems. In particular they used their efficient railway system in Prussia brilliantly.

Austria attacked Serbia on 12 August 1914, but her armies were driven back by the gallant Serbs. The Russians had already invaded East Prussia in the north and the south. The scene was set for one of the most famous battles in military history.

Using the evidence: Tannenburg

The background scene

20 August 1914. It is a stiflingly hot night at the German headquarters in Bartenstein. News has come in during the afternoon that the XX Army has suffered an unexpected defeat at Gumbinnen. Worse still, the Russian 2nd Army, led by Alexander Samsonov, has just crossed the German border. Unless

something is done quickly, the whole VIII Army will be surrounded. Disaster will strike and East Prussia may be lost. The whole German war effort could be threatened.

The decision-making
Two new commanders, Paul von Hindenberg and Erich Ludendorff, are on their way to the eastern front but a decision must be made quickly.

Divide into small groups. Carefully study all the available information. Discuss the various alternatives open to the commanders and prepare a convincing case for the decision you think they should make.

Study the map carefully before making your decisions and take account of the following information:
a) the positions of the various armies
b) the distances between the armies
c) the available means of transport
d) the physical landscape (e.g. lakes and forests)

The possible decisions
1 *Retreat:*   Withdraw all troops to the west bank of the River Vistula. Dig in here and use it as a new 'holding line'.
2 *Reinforce:*   Ask for reinforcements to be sent from the western front. Hold on until they arrive.
3 *Attack:*   Retaliate immediately against Russia's 1st Army (commanded by Rennenkampf) to stop the German army being surrounded from the north and south.
4 *Deceive:*   Draw Samsonov's 2nd Army into a trap in the south, surround it and then crush it.

Some important clues
A   The River Vistula is low in August.
B   The two Russian commanders, Rennenkampf and Samsonov, once boxed each other's ears in public. Are they still enemies?
C   Russian carelessness meant that important radio messages were often sent uncoded. Can they be trusted?
  (i) A message is intercepted on 25 August. It says that Rennenkampf cannot reach Samsonov for three days.
  (ii) Samsonov's army is marching at full speed. He broadcasts a message to say that he is going to follow the original Russian battle-plan and penetrate quickly into German territory.
D   Samsonov's army is closer to the River Vistula than most of the German troops.
E   The average speed of an army on the march is 30−50 kilometres per day. In difficult terrain, with poor roads, it may be as slow as 15−25 kilometres. The Russians have no railway transport available to them at the front line.

A map showing German East Prussia

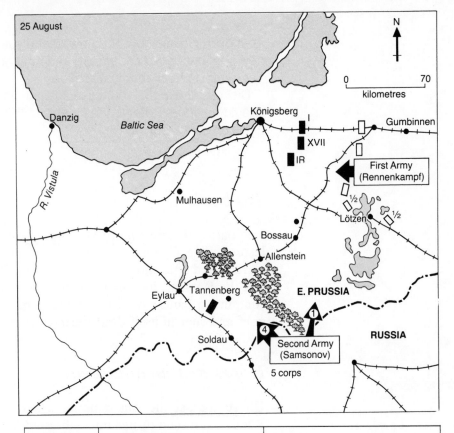

25 August

Key
-–-–- Frontier
+–+–+ Main railways
● Major towns and junctions
◗ Deep lakes
🌳 Forest
▯ Russian corps (total 9)
▮ German corps (total 4)
I▮ First German corps
½▯ Half of a Russian corps

Decision	Consequences	Clues
Consider each one in turn. Circle your first choice.	Explain what you think would be the results of each decision.	Which clues influenced your decision? Put the letter only.
1		
2		
3		
4		

23

25 August

Your decision has now been made and your plan drawn up. Your new commanders, Hindenburg and Ludendorff, have now arrived. They want to hear your justification.

Discuss and argue your case against other opinions about what should be done. Refer to the clues and the map to make your decision sound convincing.

The battle

The battle of Tannenburg was one of the most famous victories in history. The Germans surrounded the Russian 2nd Army, which surrendered after three days. Nearly 100 000 prisoners were captured and the Russians lost many of their best officers and a great deal of equipment. Samsonov, the Russian commander, was overcome with grief and shot himself dead during the retreat.

Hopes and humiliations

On 10 August the Austrians launched a massive offensive against Russia but it soon turned into a disaster. The Austrian front collapsed near Lemberg. The Austrian commander, Count Conrad, ordered a retreat that soon got out of hand and did not stop for nearly 225 kilometres. The Austrians lost 350 000 men and much valuable equipment.

In October, however, the Russians were defeated at Lodz by the Germans. At first the Russians had the upper hand; 60 000 Germans were almost surrounded and the Russians were so confident of victory that they ordered trains to be ready to take away their prisoners. But in fact the German troops managed to cut the Russian circle in two, and 16 000 Russians were eventually captured!

In December the Austrian invasion of Serbia was repelled. Even the Serbs' 70-year-old king joined the firing line in Belgrade with his rifle! By this time the war had entered a stalemate on both the western and eastern fronts. German hopes of a victory by Christmas had been smashed. A mere six months of fighting had produced over two million casualties and worse was to come.

In February 1915 another Russian offensive against Germany ended in defeat and the loss of 100 000 men. Both sides were now exhausted and no serious fighting took place on the eastern front until the spring.

THE NEW WARFARE

I can only figure it out as being something worse than the mouth of hell.

A British soldier, 1914

Trenches and technology

An early British tank crosses a trench. Note the steering gear at the rear and the anti-grenade net above

During the Great War a new and terrible kind of warfare was introduced, which brought destruction and slaughter on a scale never before seen. By 1914 science had produced deadly new weapons, better communications and the ability to manufacture greater quantities of supplies. The commanders on both sides, however, took a long time to understand these changes. They relied on old tactics, especially the open charge of massive numbers of infantrymen. They misunderstood and underestimated new weapons, such as the machine gun, tank and airplane. The result was usually hideous and devastating.

The air was vicious with bullets. . . . Ahead the clouds of smoke, sluggish low-lying fog, and fumes of bursting shells, thick in volume. . . . He blew his whistle and the company charged. They were stopped by machine-gun fire before they had passed our own entanglements. . . . The gas cylinders were still whistling and the trench full of dying men. . . .

Another soldier came crawling towards us on his belly, for all the world like a gigantic lobster . . . blood welled through his muddy khaki trousers. . . .

Quoted in A. Lloyd's book, *The War in the Trenches*, 1976

After the battle of the Marne neither Germany nor the Allies could break through their opponent's line. As a result, both sides dug trenches which eventually stretched 800 kilometres, from the Channel to the Swiss frontier. The front line trench was usually reinforced with a complicated web of support trenches, dug-outs and strong points. Some trenches were shallow but others became virtually impregnable fortresses. The German dug-outs on the Somme, for instance, were nearly 12 metres deep and were reached by underground passages. Some had electric lighting, washing equipment, surgeries, bomb-proof cellars – even steel railways for moving ammunition!

At Arras the British extended the cellars under the old castle to join up with a large underground sewer. They also enlarged caves and linked the whole system together until eventually it could hold a total of 24 000 men underground.

Bullet-proof armour. An example of the experiments that were tried out by both sides

The trench lines: an aerial sketch of the German front line, Somme 1916

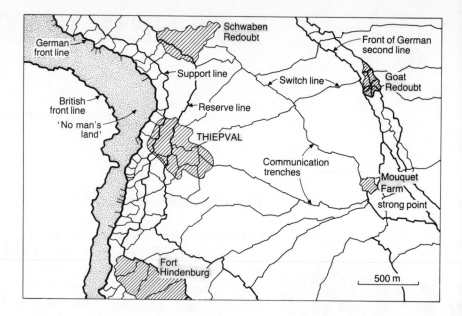

Between the two lines of trenches there was an open area – 'no man's land' – that any attacking force had to cross. Sometimes it was hundreds of metres wide; occasionally it was less than ten metres. 'No man's land' was fortified with barbed wire and machine-gun posts and was regularly patrolled by soldiers. Before long it was a wilderness of muddy shell craters, blasted trees and rotting corpses.

The big push

Continuous lines of trenches on the western front made it impossible to outflank the enemy. A decisive victory could only be gained by 'breaking out', launching a massive frontal attack on the enemy line in order to break through and into open country behind the enemy. The attackers could then 'roll' along the outflanked enemy lines.

The battle scene

Dawn. A cockerel could be heard in a nearby farm. Most of the troops were already awake, stretching and scratching cold, damp limbs. Tea was brewed over wood fires and the scent of bacon was carried towards the enemy trenches. Some soldiers still slept through the noise, huddled beneath blankets, slumped against mud walls in the crowded communication trenches. Eventually even these men were shaken from their dreams of home. Dust was brushed off crumpled tunics as a faint drizzle started to fall. The big guns stopped their pulverising fire. The soldiers' nervous conversation now sounded louder in the early morning air.

All night the artillery had pounded and battered the enemy trenches and the earth had shaken with the force of the exploding shells. It was a familiar story to the troops since it preceded every major offensive.

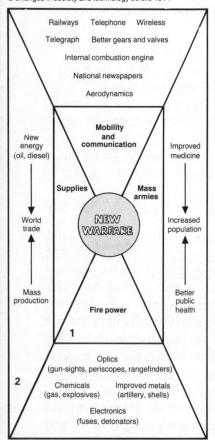

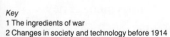

The new warfare

The hole-dwellers: British soldiers in a trench, 1916

At Loos in 1915 the artillery bombardment lasted for 96 hours. One year later, at the Somme, 2 000 heavy guns were massed on a 16-kilometre front. They fired a total of two million shells over five days. The roar was heard in London – nearly 500 kilometres away!

The shells were meant to cut the enemy's barbed wire, destroy their defences and damage the troops' morale. They usually failed. The wire was often thrown high into the air and landed in a far worse tangle than before. Trenches were usually badly damaged but often the soldiers simply took their weapons and retreated until the bombardment was over. At the Somme the Germans passed the time by playing cards in concrete bunkers deep underground. Above them British shells rained down to no real effect. However, heavy shelling did succeed in creating huge craters that slowed down the charge of the infantry. At Passchendaele in 1917 torrential rain filled the craters with muddy water. Men and horses were sucked down into their slimy depths and drowned.

Worst of all for the attackers was the simple fact that heavy artillery bombardments warned the enemy where and when a major offensive was about to begin.

Many soldiers were eventually worn down by the ear-splitting noise and the constant fear of being buried alive. It drove some men mad. A French soldier described such feelings:

We listen for an eternity to the sledgehammer beating on our trench. . . . We instantly recognise the shell that is coming to bury us. As soon as we pick out its dismal howl we look at each other in agony. All curled and shrivelled up we crouch under the very weight of its breath. Our helmets clang together, we stagger about like drunks. The beams tremble, a cloud of choking smoke fills the dug-out, the candles go out. . . .

'The Devil's Sprinkler'–the machine gun turned the war of movement into a bloody deadlock. It had the fire-power of at least 100 men

whizz-bang: the nickname given to a particular German artillery shell, because of the noise it made

Over the top

Hundreds of thousands of men got ready to charge. From a long way behind the front line they made their way to the battle front along communication trenches. Soldiers said their farewells. Many shook hands and joked, wishing each other good luck. Others prayed silently or swigged their rations of rum nervously. Crumpled snapshots of family and friends were stuffed back inside tunics or bags. Guns were slung over shoulders and equipment was hastily assembled.

Each man had to carry between 30 and 40 kilograms of gear, which made speedy movement almost impossible. All kinds of things had to be carried apart from weapons – kit, shovels, sandbags, rolls of barbed wire. At the Somme, the men of one battalion even carried large sausages by their sides to supplement their rations!

By 6.30 a.m. most soldiers had fallen silent. Suddenly the air was pierced by the sound of hundreds of whistles. At last the signal to advance had been given. Men scrambled clumsily over the top of the trenches. The swirling noise of the bagpipes could be faintly heard in the distance as a Scottish regiment marched on its enemy. The swish of bullets came all too soon. Some men were hit even as they struggled to stand up above the parapet. Their bodies slid softly back into the trench. The rest tried to advance across no man's land in strict formation – straight lines, 90 metres between each line, three paces between each man. This was intended to break the enemy lines, and most major offensives were fought in this way on the western front. Later in the war, at Verdun in 1916 and in the final offensive of 1918, the Germans used more subtle tactics. Small groups of soldiers tried to slip past the enemy front line to attack artillery positions, supply depots and even local headquarters far behind the front.

By 7 a.m. the air was thick with black, choking smoke. Shells seemed to be exploding everywhere, throwing clods of earth and human bodies high into the air. One soldier remembered:

We had no idea what it was going to be like. A few yards from the trench, a whizz-bang caught my sergeant and his head disappeared.

Bullets raced past staggering soldiers. There was a dull thud and a deep groan as a soldier 'stopped one'. Some men were hit with as many as 12 bullets before going down. The mass formation provided machine gunners with easy targets. A German soldier wrote in his diary in 1915:

Dense masses of the enemy, line after line, came into sight … advancing as if carrying out a field-day drill in peacetime. Our artillery and machine guns riddled their ranks … whole battalions must have been utterly destroyed … the massacre filled every one of us watching with a sense of disgust and nausea….

Quoted in P. Warner's book, *The Battle of Loos*, 1976

No man's land

Men looked shocked and confused but kept moving forward; training, self-discipline and bravery made sure of that. The front troops hid in shell craters until reinforcements arrived. Others simply rested; by now their packs were dead-weights. As they waited they could hear the groans and screams of wounded comrades. Cries for help rose above the sound of battle – pleas for water, for stretcher-bearers, for an end to the pain – but nobody was allowed to stop.

Some men, mad with fear and grief, turned back towards their own trenches. An officer ordered them to go forward. They refused and were shot dead by the officer.

Ahead of the attacking troops lay the fences of barbed wire. The thick wire was difficult to cut. A few gaps were made but the queues of soldiers made easy targets. In desperation some men hurled themselves at the wire. Some tried to climb over it or tugged frantically, pointlessly, at it. Most were killed.

The dead and the wounded hung like scarecrows on the wire, their torn clothing flapping in the wind. Sometimes the bodies stayed there, piled against one another, forsaken. Their bleached bones were a horrible monument to the failure of the artillery bombardment, to the stupidity of the commander's tactics, to the deadly accuracy of the enemy's guns.

Miraculously a large number got through to the enemy. They threw grenades at the machine-gun posts, wrestled with enemy soldiers, and

The hard face of war. This German soldier, like thousands on both sides, was left to rot after an artillery bombardment

British heavy howitzers on the Somme, 1916

used knives and home-made clubs. The planks some of them had carried were now thrown across enemy trenches to act as bridges.

The enemy trenches and positions might be taken, but almost certainly the enemy would counter-attack and recapture the lost ground. If the enemy did retreat it simply dug new trenches further back, faster than the attackers could advance.

Casualty figures for the 'missing', the wounded and the dead were always horribly high.

> *At dusk we all went out to get the wounded, leaving only sentries in the line. The first dead body I came upon was Samson's, hit in seventeen places. I found that he had forced his knuckles into his mouth to stop himself crying out and attracting any more men to their death.*
> Quoted in J. Simkin's book, *Contemporary Accounts of World War One*, 1982

In the spring offensive of 1918 the Germans lost 348 000 men during 40 days of fighting – nearly 10 000 men a day. The life expectancy of an inexperienced junior officer was said to be three months from the day of his recruitment. Little wonder then that there was a serious shortage of officers on both sides later in the war.

Two out of every three casualties in the Great War were the result of disease. 'Trench fever', foot rot and diarrhoea were very common complaints. Medical facilities were primitive. For example, one doctor had his surgery in a pigsty, and a casualty station of tents on the Somme in 1916 had room for 1 000 casualties but received 10 000 in the first two days of the battle.

Life in the trenches

> *... Whoever it is we are relieving, they have already gone. The trench is empty. In the watery moonlight it appears a very ghostly place. Corpses lie along the parados, rotting in the wet: every now and then a booted foot appears jutting over the trench. The wind makes it all but impassable, and now, sunk in it up to my knees, I have the momentary terror of never being able to pull myself out ... some of [the men] are already badly frost-bitten.*
> *This is the very limit of endurance.*

parados: the mound of earth and sandbags along the back of the trench

A British officer wrote this in 1916. It was his turn to take over at a front-line trench. Soldiers on both sides dreaded the prospect of a return to trench life, enduring conditions that one soldier compared to being 'eye deep in hell'. Exhaustion, poor hygiene and fear were the unbeatable enemies. A French soldier said: 'You eat, you drink, you sleep in the midst of dying. You laugh and sing in the company of corpses.'

Here is a typical monthly rota for an army division (a unit of about 20 000 soldiers).

4 days in front.
4 days in support.
8 days in reserve.
Remainder for resting behind the lines,
in tents, farm buildings or local villages
and towns.

There were cases, however, where soldiers were forced to spend two months at the front line without relief.

Using the evidence: a year in the trenches
Historians use different types of evidence to build up accurate pictures of past events. Study the evidence below. Can you use it to find out what life was like in the trenches during 1916?

A   The diary of a soldier

Jan. 8–9   *Left Rouen and had a very tedious journey. Arrived in the early hours of morning at Pont Remy and marched to a place . . . where we had some hard training!*

Jan. 18   *Played the 2nd Gordons at football and beat them 4–3 after a very hard game.*

Feb. 1   *In the evening helped to extinguish a fire at a cotton mill at Picquigny.*

Feb. 25   *Left Ville-sur-Corbie and marched about 8 klms. We then got into buses and eventually arrived at Longueau, just outside Amiens, about 4 p.m. A snowstorm had raged all the day, and nearly everybody was frozen stiff.*
At 8 p.m. we entrained, and arrived at Hazebrouck about 8 the following morning. We then marched to Wallon Cappel.

March 7   *Marched to Boësgheim.*

March 24   *Marched to Vieux Berquin.*

April 7   *In the trenches to the left of Neuve Chapelle, Lance Sgt. Buxton killed by a sniper, who was firing from a tree.*

May 3   *We are only a few yards from the Germans. Only this morning one of the enemy shouted 'Chuck us a tin of jam over, Tommy!' One of our chaps looking over was shot through the eye.*

May 9   *. . . A mine also exploded on our right towards the brick-fields on the other side of the canal. At this place we had fish for tea for when the shell exploded in the canal the fish floated to the top.*

June 13	Raining in torrents. Everybody wet through. If it rains much more we shall have to swim for it.
June 21	We have started a bugle band and a drum and fife band.
July 2	During the morning we visited the village, where there was hardly a house standing. . . . We visited the graveyard, where there were some terrible sights. Shells had dropped all about and you could see the bones of people who had been buried for years.
Sept. 2	Weather very hot. Bombardment still continues.
Sept. 3	Zero. At last the guns crash. Hell! what a row. You can't hear yourself speak. What an inferno! Wherever you look you see shells bursting. . . . The sky is one mass of flames. . . . The first wave goes over. What a sight! Men being mowed down like ninepins. . . .
Sept. 16	The rats are quite a pest here. We have to hang our rations on lines. . . . They are a very hungry lot, as one of them bit the nose of one of our men whilst he was asleep.
Sept. 20	Back to rest billets.
Nov. 6	Rejoined my unit after leave. Terrible weather – mud, mud, mud, once more up to the neck in it.
Dec. 25	Christmas Day, not in the workhouse, but in the trenches, which is worse still.

billets: local houses and barns in which soldiers were allowed to stay

Sgt. James Boardman, Cheshire Regiment, 1916

B   A photograph of a British trench, 1916

C   A photograph of a German underground dug-out, 1916

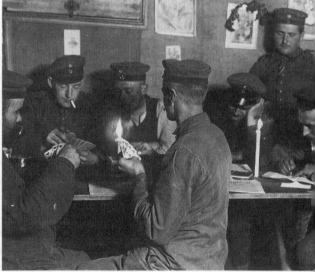

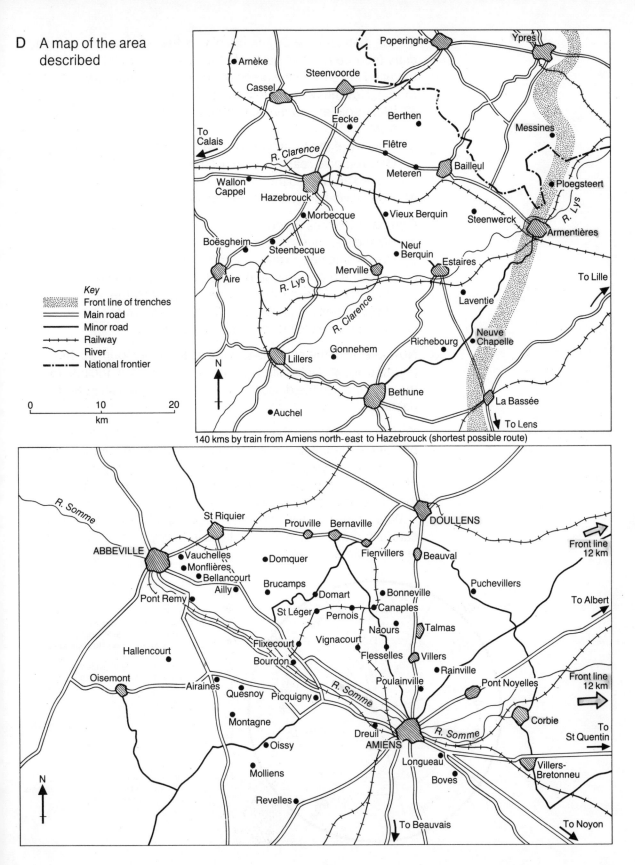

D A map of the area described

Key
- Front line of trenches
- Main road
- Minor road
- Railway
- River
- National frontier

0 10 20
km

Top map:
To Calais
To Lille
To Lens
Arnèke
Steenvoorde
Cassel
Eecke
Berthen
Flêtre
Meteren
Bailleul
Poperinghe
Ypres
Messines
Ploegsteert
R. Clarence
Wallon Cappel
Hazebrouck
Morbecque
Vieux Berquin
Steenwerck
Armentières
R. Lys
Boësgheim
Steenbecque
Merville
Neuf Berquin
Estaires
Aire
R. Lys
Laventie
Gonnehem
R. Clarence
Richebourg
Neuve Chapelle
Lillers
Bethune
La Bassée
Auchel

140 kms by train from Amiens north-east to Hazebrouck (shortest possible route)

Bottom map:
R. Somme
St Riquier
Prouville
Bernaville
DOULLENS
Front line 12 km
To Albert
ABBEVILLE
Vauchelles
Monflières
Bellancourt
Domquer
Fienvillers
Beauval
Puchevillers
Pont Remy
Ailly
Brucamps
Domart
Bonneville
St Léger
Pernois
Canaples
Talmas
Naours
Flixecourt
Vignacourt
Villers
Hallencourt
Bourdon
Flesselles
Rainville
Front line 12 km
Oisemont
Airaines
Quesnoy
Picquigny
R. Somme
Poulainville
Pont Noyelles
To St Quentin
Montagne
Dreuil
R. Somme
Corbie
Oissy
AMIENS
Longueau
Villers-Bretonneu
Molliens
Boves
Revelles
To Beauvais
To Noyon

N

33

1 On the map (source **D**) find the places that are mentioned in the diary (source **A**), then calculate the distances that this soldier travelled in 1916 (use a piece of string for measuring winding roads). Now answer the following questions:
   a) Were soldiers always stationed in one part of the fighting front?
   b) How were the troops moved from one place to another?
   c) Can you give reasons to explain why these troops were moved around so much?
   d) How typical do you think this soldier's year was?

2 Compare sources **B** and **C**.
   a) What differences can you see?
   b) How would you explain these differences?
   c) Does the diary (source **A**) agree or disagree with the evidence of life in the trenches provided by the photographs? Refer to specific factual information in the three sources to support your conclusions.

3 Now use all of the sources to write as full an account as the sources allow of what life was like in the trenches. Include (a) the dangers, (b) the discomforts, and (c) the pleasures and pastimes.

4 Your account of trench life and warfare has been based on primary evidence. It is not adequate, however, because (a) it is only about the year 1916, and (b) it is based on only three types of historical source – a diary, photographs and a map. You therefore have gaps in your account.

   What evidence will help to fill these gaps? Study the diagram carefully. Some of it has been filled in. Copy it into your book and complete the rest.

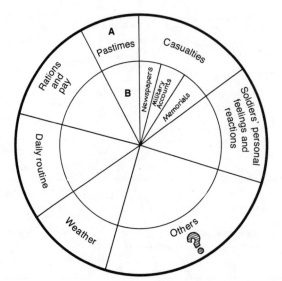

A: The headings in this circle cover aspects of trench life that you, as a historian, need to know about.

B: The main types of evidence that will help the historian.

  1 Diaries
  2 Newspapers
  3 Private letters
  4 Military records, plans and memos
  5 Maps
  6 Tunics and equipment
  7 Weapons
  8 Pay books
  9 Battlegrounds and buildings
10 Memorial statues and monuments
11 Poetry and paintings

DEADLOCK, 1915-17

Yes, I am still very keen but such slaughter as is going on these days seems to be wrong. . . . Why must we throw so many noble lives away as if they were dirt.

Letter from a British officer, 1916

In 1915 both sides looked for a new solution to the stalemate of 1914. It was to prove to be a crucial year. The Germans now realised it was going to be a long war and switched their main offensive to the eastern front. Their western armies went on the defensive, strengthening trench lines and trying to hold ground. The Allies, on the other hand, were determined to attack and to drive German troops out of all occupied territory, especially the rich industrial area of northern France. Their offensives were therefore concentrated in the Artois and Champagne regions.

Both sides still believed a decisive victory could be achieved. They increased the size of their armies with volunteers and persuaded other countries to join in. In April Italy entered on the side of the Allies; Turkey and Bulgaria joined the Central Powers (in October 1914 and September 1915). The year turned out to be one of deadlock – the pattern for the next three years.

From Champagne to gas: the major offensives of 1915 on the western front

Time of year	Area	Main attacking army	The battle	Achievement of objectives	
				Success	Failure
March	Champagne	F	Cost 90 000 French casualties – gained only 8 kilometres.		X
March	Neuve Chapelle	B	Ran out of artillery shells; took Germans by surprise but in the end lost 12 000 British men – gained $2\frac{1}{2}$ square kilometres.		X
April	Ypres	G	First use of poisonous chlorine gas – opened 8 kilometre gap in the Allied line but eventually gap closed up.		X
May and Sept.	Vimy Ridge	F	700 000 shells used; high ground captured at a cost of 100 000 French casualties.		X
Sept.	Loos	B	British troops poisoned by own gas; broke through up to 5 kilometres into German territory but lost it eventually. (John French sacked and replaced by Douglas Haig.)		X

B = British   F = French   G = German

Many smaller actions took place along the western front, without much success. Despite the optimism of the generals, 1915 ended badly. A German wrote at the time:

> *Enthusiasm is dying bit by bit. . . . That is what distinguished this war – on all fronts . . . the feeling of insufficiency. No one has strength enough.*

Russia's collapse and recovery

The Germans launched a major offensive against Russia on the eastern front in the spring of 1915. They wanted to recapture the salient (land surrounded by enemies on three sides) that jutted into Polish and Austrian territory. The Russian line was bombarded by the biggest artillery attack ever seen on the eastern front. About 1 000 guns crushed the Russian defences and the Germans achieved a spectacular breakthrough. They advanced 144 kilometres and the whole Russian front in that area collapsed. Warsaw fell to the Germans in August and a million rounds of precious ammunition were captured.

Throughout the summer the Russian army was forced to retreat. At Przemyśl 120 000 prisoners were taken. This utter collapse helped to destroy morale permanently among the Russian troops and among citizens at home. The Russian war-machine was a great tottering giant that was bled to death for three years. It outnumbered the Germans' eastern army by four to one and yet it was always outmanoeuvred. In 1915 Russia suffered one million casualties, one million men were taken prisoner and over 3 000 pieces of artillery were abandoned.

Brusilov's offensive

Astonishingly, in 1916 Russia recovered enough to win its greatest victory of the war. In June the Russian commander Brusilov launched a massive attack on the Austrian positions in Galicia. He advanced on a 1 126-kilometre front and achieved stunning success. The Austrians deserted in their thousands. By 18 June 350 000 Austrians and more than 500 artillery guns had been captured. At certain points Brusilov's army penetrated 112 kilometres into Austrian-held territory.

For a tantalising moment it seemed that Russia had a unique opportunity of winning the war on the eastern front. Another Russian army, two million strong, was assembled on the German frontier but did not attack because of poor communications between the two armies.

By October, 35 German divisions had been brought from the western front to reinforce the Austrian line. Rumania's entry into the war (in August) and attack on Austria came too late to help the Brusilov offensive. The chance of decisive victory had gone. A deadlock developed over the whole eastern front.

The dangers of gas could be overcome with masks. By 1918, 63 different kinds of poisonous chemicals had been used on the western front

Six months later, in March 1917, a revolution exploded inside Russia. It was caused by a number of things – weariness of the fighting, disgust with the corruption of the Russian leaders, starvation of the population. The Revolution eventually ended the Russian war effort. On 3 March 1918, Russia and Germany signed a peace treaty at Brest Litovsk. This turn of events saved Austria from total collapse – it had suffered five million casualties and lost huge areas of its territory. It also allowed Germany to concentrate on the western front, where the deadlock had continued.

Using the evidence: hidden messages

In Command

Our Officer

A British postcard	B Secret message
It was dangerous to publicly express anti-war feelings. Above you can see one method of getting around the problem.	The sketch above is not as simple and innocent as it first appears. It contains the name and date of a future battle. (i) The name is of a town. It has five letters. (ii) The date is the '8th' (8, T, H). Can you find where this information is hidden?
Your solution of puzzle a) Meaning? b) Why did the publishers call themselves 'The Cynicus Publishing Company'?	Your solution of puzzle a) Name of town? b) Where is the date hidden?

1916: a year of blood

For the generals on the western front, 1916 began and ended in frustration. In between, two major offensives were launched. They produced a total of one-and-a-half-million dead, wounded or missing. Battles in other war areas had not produced the victory that the generals and politicians had hoped for. Both Falkenhayn and Haig now believed that the Great War could only be won on the western front, so even larger armies with more powerful artillery were thrown into battle. Both sides believed that a decisive 'break out' through enemy lines was possible. Certainly the troops of 1916 were the best that the war produced, as the volunteer soldiers who had survived were now experienced in warfare.

Size of armies in 1916			
Allies		*Central Powers*	
British	3 516 000	Germany	5 470 000
French	2 978 000	Austria	2 750 000
Russian	4 767 000	Turkey	500 000
Others	2 576 000	Bulgaria	400 000
	13 837 000		9 120 000

A massive offensive was planned by the Allies for the summer. The Germans, however, beat them to it.

Verdun

Falkenhayn decided to try to destroy the French army at Verdun and thereby force the British to surrender. He chose to attack Verdun mainly because it controlled a vital route to Paris.

The battle turned into one of the most bloody of the whole war. It soon earned itself nicknames – 'the mincing machine' and 'the hell of Verdun'. Between March and July 1 200 heavy German guns fired 24 million shells. Most soldiers who died never even saw the enemy.

The whole salient smelled of poisonous gas and decomposed bodies. One soldier remembered how it was:

You found the dead embedded in the walls of the trenches; heads, legs and half-bodies, just as they had been shovelled out of the way by the picks and shovels of the working party.

By the end of February the French were near to collapse. They made Henri Philippe Pétain Commander-in-Chief in place of Joffre, reorganised their defences and sent reinforcements. In one week in

The walking wounded. A German soldier is captured at the Somme

March 190 000 men marched along the main route from Paris – 'The Sacred Way' as the French called it. After ten months the Germans called off the campaign because the British had begun a huge attack on their line further north. Verdun cost Germany 280 000 casualties and the French 315 000 casualties.

The Somme

On 1 July Haig, the British Commander-in-Chief, launched his first major offensive of the war near the River Somme. He wanted to relieve the French at Verdun and show his troops 'that Germany was not invincible on the western front'. His plan had fatal weaknesses, however. The Germans had the high ground, for instance, and the British army's massive artillery bombardment, which lasted for five days, did not cut the German wire as Haig believed it would. Throughout the spring the Germans expected an attack and reinforced their positions.

Hopes were high in the British ranks – cages were even built to hold future German prisoners – but these hopes were not fulfilled. By the end of the first day 60 000 British soldiers had been killed, wounded or taken prisoner. They were the worst casualties in British military history. Three-quarters of the officers were wiped out. Some battalions were almost totally destroyed in a few hours as wave after wave of men were sent out to almost certain death. For months Haig persisted with the campaign. Territory was eventually captured, but the Germans poured reinforcements in to try to hold every metre of ground. Both sides suffered a massive number of casualties. For example, 80 000 British soldiers died in the campaign to capture Delville Wood. In September a small number of tanks were used by Britain for the first time. They were supposed to capture the Pozières ridge but got stuck in the winter mud.

By the end of the year the Germans had been brought to the point of total collapse. Falkenhayn was replaced by Erich Ludendorff. It was the worst crisis that the Germans had to face before their final defeat in 1918. Bad weather intervened in November, however, and the British army was also exhausted. The battle of the Somme was one of the most controversial in military history.

Using the evidence: slaughter on the Somme

Haig has been bitterly criticised for allowing the battle to continue after the opening disaster. Some thought his actions were stubborn, stupid and inhuman. It is said that 'the flower of British youth' was cut down for no real purpose. His supporters argue that this was the high price of victory. But did the battle of the Somme achieve its specific aims? And was the campaign worthwhile overall?

Haig's aims

1 To 'break out' and capture territory, such as:

   a position on the Pozières ridge extending from the vicinity of Montauben to the River Ancre, so as to secure good observation over the ground to the eastward of that ridge.

   a good position [near] the River Ancre . . . so as to cover the left flank of the operations south of that river.

2 To relieve the French at Verdun and prevent their total collapse.

3 To inflict heavy losses on the Germans and wear them down.

The evidence
1 Captured territory

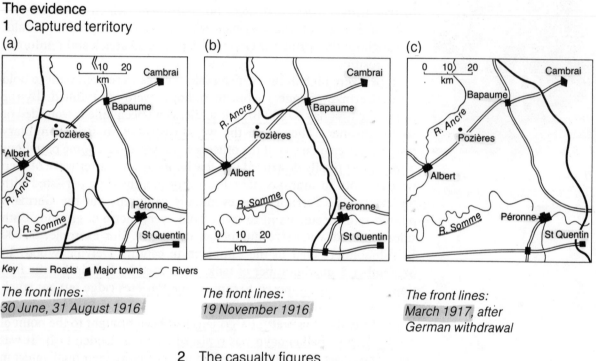

(a)

The front lines:
30 June, 31 August 1916

(b)

The front lines:
19 November 1916

(c)

The front lines:
March 1917, after German withdrawal

Key ══ Roads ▪ Major towns ⌇ Rivers

2 The casualty figures

Britain	France	Germany
400 000 (1st day: 60 000)	200 000	600 000

. . . The endurance of the troops had been weakened by long spells of defence under the powerful enemy artillery fire. . . . We were completely exhausted on the Western Front.

The Somme was the muddy grave of the German field army.

Erich Ludendorff,
the German Commander-in-Chief in 1918

3 Verdun
   The Germans were forced to switch thousands of their troops from Verdun to the Somme. This took pressure off the French.

1 Study maps (a) and (b), then compare them with Haig's aims. Did the British achieve Haig's ambitions?
2 Study map (c), then consider the two opinions below. Which do you agree with and why?
   Opinion 1: 'This is the price of victory.'
   Opinion 2: 'It proves the ground was not worth fighting for.'
3 Look at the casualty figures and then consider the following points:
   (i) The Germans calculated their casualty total every ten days, whereas the British added up the numbers daily.
   (ii) The Germans did not record lightly wounded or missing soldiers as casualties, whereas the British figures included all wounded, dead and missing soldiers.
       a) Explain why the real German casualty figures may have been far higher than those published.
       b) Does your answer to 3a support the opinions of Ludendorff on page 40?
4 Consider all the evidence. Was the slaughter on the Somme worthwhile? Give reasons for your answer.

1917: no breakthrough

The 'wearing-out' strategy of the generals had resulted in heavy loss of life. 1917 therefore saw the search for, in Haig's words, 'the eventual decisive blow'. No such thing happened. The year saw more blood-letting and no decisive breakthrough. The reasons were quite clear. In the first place, the offensives began too late. The winter of 1916–17 was one of the worst in European history, and it slowed down all Allied preparations for a new campaign. Secondly, the new German Commander-in-Chief, Erich Ludendorff, confused the British by withdrawing all his troops to a new front line – 'the Hindenberg Line'. The purpose of this bold and clever move was to gain time for his weary armies until the German U-boats had starved Britain out of the war (see page 51). On average the Germans withdrew 30 kilometres along a 105-kilometre front. They ruthlessly destroyed the area they surrendered; villages were flattened and roads ripped up, orchards were burnt and wells poisoned. They retreated so quietly that it was days before the British realised they had gone!

The most important reason for the Allies' lack of success in 1917 was the unimaginative thinking of their commanders. They did not seem to learn the lessons of more than two years of futile slaughter.

The major offensives of 1917 on the western front

Date	Area	Main attacking army	The battle	Achievement of objectives	
				Success	Failure
April	Arras	B	Canadians captured Vimy Ridge, but lost $\frac{1}{10}$ of their total force. Failed to penetrate the Hindenberg Line.	X	X
April–May	St. Quentin	F	Nivelle, France's new commander, planned mass attack – but wire not cut and Germans knew of attack in advance. 187 000 French casualties for 5 kilometres of ground.		X
June	Messines Ridge	B	450 tons of explosive in underground mine help capture high ground.	X	
August–November	Ypres (3rd Battle) (a) Passchendaele	B	Appalling wet weather and muddy conditions – $4\frac{1}{2}$ million shells in first 10 days – main aim of 'break-out' near Ypres failed – 245 000 casualties for 11 kilometres of ground.		X
November	(b) Cambrai	B	Tanks used successfully for first time – 8 kilometres advance on $9\frac{1}{2}$-kilometre front and 10 000 prisoners captured – Germans recaptured ground.		X

B = British   F = French

DIFFERENT DIMENSIONS

The Great War added new dimensions to warfare. By 1915 men were fighting in the air, underground and even beneath the oceans.

Birds of prey

In 1914 aircraft were used in warfare on a large scale for the first time. Initially, pilots dropped grenades on enemy trenches, but later the technical quality of the aircraft improved dramatically and German planes were able to drop 1000 kilogram bombs on British cities.

At the beginning of the war nobody really expected aircraft to play a large part in the actual fighting. The pilot's main job was to observe the enemy – the position of the trenches and artillery, the size of the army, the movement of troops and supplies. Photographs, wireless messages and written reports helped to provide valuable information for the commanders. Soon, however, aircraft were used to stop the enemy going on these vital spying missions. Fighter aircraft were designed and squadrons were formed. A race soon began to produce superior fighter aircraft – the new birds of prey.

Each new improvement by one side was quickly matched by changes in the enemy's aircraft and tactics. Supremacy in the air switched from one side to the other throughout the war. Overall, the Germans probably produced the more skilful pilots and the better aircraft, especially the Fokker E-III and the Albatross DIII. However, the British Sopwith Camel was probably the most successful fighter of the war. It shot down 1294 enemy machines.

The German fighter pilots cleverly organised themselves in flying groups known as 'Circuses' and 'Jastas'. Some Germans printed their names in enormous letters on the upper wing so that their opponents would recognise them and be frightened. One German pilot even added after his name: 'Do you not remember me?'

The killing time
Air-fighting during the Great War was both exciting and deadly dangerous. This is what a British pilot wrote about it:

The way the earth looked, falling; swallowing to stop deafness at altitude; the scream of wires; stars between wings; grass blown down when engines were run up; the smell – of dope, and castor oil, and varnish in new cockpits; moonlight shining on struts; the gasps before the diving; machine guns.

dope: a thick liquid used as a lubricant

Quoted in A. Clark's book, *Aces High*, 1973

A 'circus' of German Albatross fighters at their airbase. Note the tent hangers in the background. The second aircraft is said to be that of Manfred von Richthofen, the most successful pilot of the war. The 'Red Baron' was eventually shot down in 1918

In 1914 equipment was primitive. Airplanes were flimsy affairs, made out of canvas, timber and piano wire. Hand pistols were used by pilots and some even threw grenades at each other. One desperate German pilot was reported to have tried to throw a brick! Later on, machine guns were mounted in fixed positions and the fighting gained a grisly glamour as a sport for gentlemen warriors.

Better equipment and weapons introduced in 1915 changed air-fighting into a serious and deadly science. It was called 'the killing time' by the top German pilot Manfred von Richthofen. By 1917 a young pilot could expect to live for only 11 days from the time of his arrival in France. One pilot wrote to his family: 'There have been two changes in the bunk next to me since April Fool's Day (last week!). I wouldn't sleep in it for all the tea in China.' Many new pilots were so inexperienced that they lost control of their aircraft and spun to their death before even facing the enemy in combat.

Certain pilots became famous because of their success in the air. The German pilot Werner Voss shot down 22 British planes in 21 days. Such men were known as 'aces' and their number of 'kills' was reported eagerly by the press in each country. They became public celebrities, idolised by civilians. One ace, Albert Ball, wrote about his feelings:

Huns: nickname for the Germans, implying that they were barbaric

Oh it was a good fight, and the Huns were fine sports. One tried to ram me, after he was hit, and only missed by inches. Am indeed looked after by God, but oh! I do get tired of living always to kill, and am really beginning to feel like a murderer. Shall be so pleased when I have finished.

Quoted in A. Clark's book, *Aces High*, 1973

Ball, who shot down 43 German planes, was killed before he was 21 years old. Very few aces survived the war; they were victims of engine failure, jammed guns or, simply, better opponents.

Ace	Official number of 'kills'	Nationality
Edward 'Mick' Mannock	73 (top British ace)	British
William 'Billy' Bishop	72	Canadian
René Fonck	75 (top Allied ace)	French
Georges Guynemer	54	French
Manfred von Richthofen, the 'Red Baron'	80 (top war ace)	German
Ernst Udet	62	German
Godwin Brunowski	40	Austrian

Casualties in the air on the western front		
	Germans	Allies
Killed	5 853	6 166
Wounded	7 302	7 245
Missing or taken prisoner	275	3 212

The bombers

The Great War also saw the beginning of 'strategic bombing' in the destruction of military and civilian targets by air attack. From now onwards even civilians at home could become fatal victims of wars being fought far away. By 1918 German Gotha aircraft were dropping bombs on targets over 500 kilometres away in the south-east of England, especially London.

As early as January 1915, however, bombing raids were being carried out by large airships, called Zeppelins, which caused a lot of panic but were not very effective. They made 202 attacks and killed a total of 556 people, injuring a further 1 358.

By 1917 the airships had been replaced by German multi-engined airplanes such as the Gothas and the 'Giants'. The British produced the Handly Page V/1500 with a wingspan of nearly 40 metres.

Although the bombers did not do a great deal of damage to property, people were frightened by the raids. The night shifts in munition factories, for instance, were badly disrupted. On some nights, whether there was a raid or not, 300 000 Londoners sheltered in the underground railway stations. By the end of 1916 more than 17 000 men and 110 aircraft were involved in the air defence of Britain. Better anti-aircraft guns were developed and 'night fighters' began to use 'tracer' and incendiary bullets. More powerful searchlights and explosive balloons also helped to keep enemy bombers at bay.

The war underground

As both sides struggled to break the deadlock an ancient method of fighting was revived – mining. By 1915 special 'sapper' units were tunnelling beneath the enemy trenches to lay high explosives. The early mines were small but by 1917 it was a very different story. Records show that at Messines Ridge 11 mining teams fired 19 separate mines 'with a total of one million pounds of explosive'. One of the tunnels was 38 metres deep and 503 metres long!

The war underground became a separate, almost private, battle. In appalling conditions the 'moles', as they called themselves, scratched away at the chalk or clay soil under French and Belgian fields. Tunnels were narrow, dark and damp. Men worked in shifts of eight hours, stripped naked to the waist. Sometimes the tunnellers would come across enemy tunnels and had to fight it out, deep underground.

The soldiers in the trenches lived in fear of the underground mines. They rammed sticks into the muddy ground and held the upper ends between their teeth to feel the vibrations of underground digging. The blasts usually came suddenly, without warning and with devastating effects. An eye-witness described the spectacular explosion at Messines in 1917:

> *Out of the dark ridges . . . there gushed out and up enormous volumes of scarlet flame from the exploding mines and of earth and smoke all lighted by the flame spilling over into fountains of fierce colour, so that all the countryside was illuminated by red light. Where some of us stood watching, aghast and spellbound by this burning horror, the ground crumbled and surged violently to and fro. Truly the earth quaked . . . .*
>
> Quoted in A. Barrie's book, *War Underground*, 1981

Overall, the war underground was not as successful as the commanders had hoped it would be and it was called off in 1917. It took too much effort to create a limited number of explosions. Also, mining activity produced huge quantities of earth which attracted the shells of the enemy's artillery. Troops in the trenches disliked the miners because of this.

The war at sea

Freedom of the seas was very important for both sides during the Great War. The military effort depended on vast supplies of food, equipment and raw materials. Britain in particular imported a high percentage of its vital supplies by sea. In 1914, however, very few people understood what the war at sea was to be like. Technology had provided new vessels of great power. One *Dreadnought*-type battleship, for instance, was reckoned to have the fire power of a whole

In 1915 the sinking of the passenger ship, the Lusitania, *by the Germans, outraged the world. The loss of 128 Americans aboard also helped to persuade the USA to join the war two years later*

division of land troops. New artillery and improved range-finding equipment meant that battles could be fought between enemy ships that were more than 16 kilometres apart. Seaplanes and submarines created new threats from above and below. The newly invented wireless, and the use of airships for spying, meant that enemy positions could be tracked. Most sinister of all was the new ruthlessness. The Germans attacked supply vessels and civilian ships without any warning. On 22 September 1914, one German U-boat sank three British cruisers, despite the fact that two of the ships were simply trying to pick up survivors from the third.

The waiting game

Neither Britain nor Germany was willing to risk losing their battle-fleet in a major battle. To lose access to the sea would be to lose the war. As a result there were very few major naval clashes. The German High Seas Fleet stayed safely in port behind underwater minefields for most of the war. They left it to their submarines to attack the British battle-fleet and merchant vessels. However, one big battle and several minor ones did take place.

47

Date	Place of engagement	Outcome
1 Nov. 1915	Coronel	German battlecruisers sank two British ships and killed 1 000 men.
8 Dec. 1915	Falkland Islands	Six German warships (2 000 men) sunk by *Invincible* and *Inflexible*.
24 Jan. 1916	Dogger Bank	German war fleet trapped by British Grand Fleet, but escaped with the loss of only two warships.
31 May 1916	Jutland	Largest naval battle of the war (259 warships carrying 100 000 men); 25 warships and 9 000 lives were lost. Both sides later claimed a victory.

Using the evidence: Jutland – the victory that never was?

A Background information

(i) The plan

Admiral Scheer planned to trap and destroy some of the main ships in the British fleet. He intended using submarines, Zeppelins and the main German battle-fleet. Five German battlecruisers, commanded by Admiral Hipper, were to act as bait to lure Admiral Beatty's six cruisers to sea. The main German fleet was to wait unseen 64 kilometres to the south, ready to attack. It would then destroy Beatty's ships before the rest of the main British fleet could arrive. Unknown to the Germans, the British had intercepted messages and knew about the German plan.

(ii) The engagement
31 May

2.20 p.m.	The fleets make contact.
3.45 p.m.	Beatty fires on Hipper. A fierce battle results in five British destroyers being sunk. Beatty exclaims: 'There seems to be something wrong with our bloody ships today.' Both Hipper and Beatty try to lure the enemy towards their own main fleets.
4.33 p.m.	The main German fleet arrives and unknowingly chases Beatty towards Admiral Jellicoe's main British battle-fleet.
6.45 p.m.	The main fleets clash but only for a few minutes. Heavy punishing fire from the British 380-millimetre shells (weighing nearly one tonne each) forces Scheer's fleet to turn away and make a run for safety.

7.12 p.m. The main German fleet turns eastward and, in so doing, is outmanoeuvred by the British. Again they run into the firing line of Jellicoe's ships.

In the fading light the German fleet breaks through the tail of the British fleet. The German ships have flares and searchlights which allow them to escape the British in the darkness. The Germans race to port and safety.

1 June

5 a.m. The German fleet made for harbour to repair vessels. They never again risked a major battle.

B The casualties

(i) Ships lost

Type	British	German
Battleships	—	1
Battlecruisers	3	1
Cruisers	3	4
Destroyers	8	5
Total tonnage lost	112 000	61 000

(ii) Men lost

	British	German
Dead	6 097	2 551
Wounded	510	507
Captured	177	—

C The size of the fleets at the battle

	British	German
Battleships	28	22
Battlecruisers	9	5
Cruisers (light and armoured)	34	11
Destroyers	80	61

D The aims of the two fleets

(i) Both sides intended to trap their opponents.

(ii) The British wanted to inflict maximum damage on the whole German battle-fleet.

(iii) The Germans wanted to destroy only a small number of British vessels.

E A diagram showing the main points in the battle

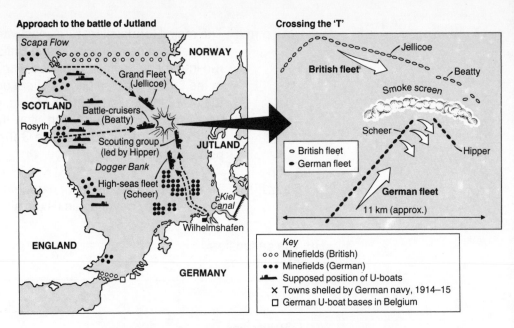

Approach to the battle of Jutland

Crossing the 'T'

Key
- ○○○ Minefields (British)
- ●●● Minefields (German)
- ⚓ Supposed position of U-boats
- ✕ Towns shelled by German navy, 1914–15
- ☐ German U-boat bases in Belgium

1 Afterwards both sides claimed a victory. Use the story of the battle and the evidence above to answer the following questions:

a) Why was there doubt about who had won?

b) Who do *you* think won the battle of Jutland?

2 Copy out and complete the following chart. Study the evidence carefully and then circle the appropriate answer.

	British	German	Equal	Sources to consult
Who lost most – a) ships? .... b) tonnage? ...... c) men?	(B) (B) (B)	G G G	E E E	B
Who lost the greatest percentage of their ships?	(B)	G	E	B and C
Which of the two sides gave up?	B	(G)	E	A (ii) and E
Did the two sides achieve their aims? Aim (i) .... Aim (ii) .... Aim (iii)	(Yes) (Yes) (Yes)	(No) (No) (No)	Uncertain Uncertain Uncertain	A (ii), B, C and D

3 A controversial debate
   Discuss the following issues in groups of two or four. Take both
   the German and British side. The table and the evidence will
   help you.
   a) 'Tonnage is more important than the number of ships sunk
      when calculating which side lost most.'
      Do you agree? Give your reasons.
   b) 'The original size of the fleets makes a big difference to a
      decision about who lost most.'
      Is this true? Explain your answer.
   c) 'The fact that the Germans retreated means that they were
      defeated.'
      How far is this opinion justified?

The invisible enemy

Submarine warfare nearly won the war for Germany. They began a
full-scale campaign against Allied merchant shipping in February
1915. Two years later they declared 'unrestricted warfare' on *all*
vessels suspected of helping the enemy. The new policy of 1917 was
meant to stop the blockade of German ports by British warships. The
submarines were also meant to break the deadlock on the western
front by cutting off the Allied armies' vital supplies and by starving
the British population into surrender.

In the beginning submarine warfare was very successful. In August
1915, one single U-boat sank 30 ships during a 25-day expedition. In
April 1917, Britain lost over 300 ships. The number of neutral ships
visiting British ports fell by 75 per cent. It was reckoned that Britain
only had six weeks' supply of corn left!

Why then didn't the Germans win the naval war at this stage? The
reasons are given below in the form of a diagram.

*How the U-boat menace
was overcome*

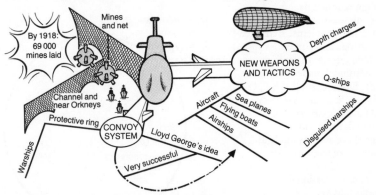

The morale of the U-boat crews slumped. Unrestricted submarine
warfare had brought the powerful United States into the war and the
Allied blockade of German ports had brought near starvation in
Germany. The German plan had backfired disastrously.

Other fronts

'Easterners' versus 'Westerners'

By 1915 the war had spread from northern Europe to other fronts. Some British politicians (known as 'Easterners') wanted to try to break the deadlock on the western front by defeating the Central Powers in the east and south of Europe. They hoped to create vital supply routes to Russia and also to encourage neutral countries such as Italy, Bulgaria and Rumania to join the Allies.

Their opponents (known as 'Westerners') said that even if these things were achieved Germany would *still* have to be defeated on the western front.

The Gallipoli disaster

In 1915 a daring British plan to capture Constantinople, defeat Turkey and attack Austria through the Balkans failed miserably. The campaign used naval bombardments and Allied landings but the brave soldiers were poorly commanded, badly organised and never received the necessary supplies from home. It failed to achieve any of its aims in ten months and cost the lives of over 40 000 Allied troops. It ended hopes of a southern route to Russia and brought down the British government at home.

The main campaigns

Soldiers on these other fronts faced terrible problems. Extreme temperatures, and almost impossible terrain (mountains, desert or jungle) made fighting difficult. Diseases such as malaria, cholera and dysentery caused far more casualties than the actual fighting did. Inexperienced natives made up the majority of troops in Africa and Arabia, led by small numbers of professional European soldiers.

In Africa the Allies conquered German colonies one by one – Togoland and the Cameroons (1914), South-West Africa (1915) and German East Africa (1917).

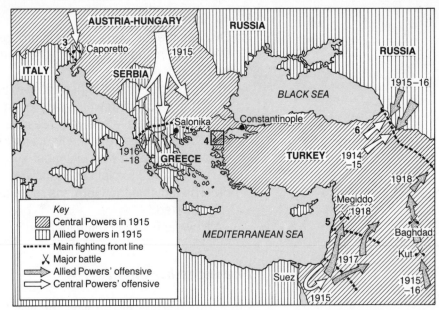

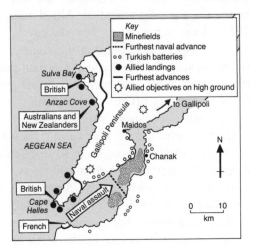

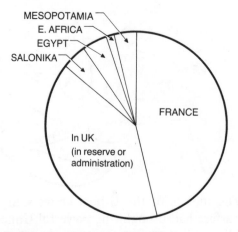

British troops at war: 4.3 million troops around the world

Front	Main troops
1 Western	British, French, German
2 Eastern	German, Austrian, Russian
3 Southern	Italian, Austrian
4 Balkan	British, French, ANZAC (Australians and New Zealanders), Austrian, Turkish, Russian, Serbian, Bulgarian
5 Middle East	British, French, Turkish, Arabs
6 Caucasian	Turkish, Russian
7 African	British, German, Africans

NATIONS AT WAR

The Government cannot win without you.

David Lloyd George, 1915

Total war

Hardly anybody in Europe escaped the effects of the Great War. More than 65 million people went to war as soldiers. Many of the civilians at home also contributed to the war by their work in the munitions factories or by producing military clothing and equipment. Many millions more were affected indirectly by food shortages, by the destruction of houses and property and by new government regulations. The Great War was a battle of entire nations. It was fought not only with guns but with farms, factories and newspapers. For every soldier, there were three civilian workers keeping him supplied. The war effort cost the British government some £7 852 million! Personal taxation rose from 6 p. in the pound to 30 p. to help pay for it.

Governments were forced to take greater control of the nation in order to make the war effort efficient. In Britain the Defence of the Realm Act (DORA) was passed in 1914. It gave the government enormous powers and affected people's everyday lives. Below is a list of some of these measures:

1 The coal mines were nationalised.
2 The railways were controlled by the government.
3 Newspapers, books and letters were censored.
4 British Summer Time was invented and clocks were put forward by one hour to 'save' daylight.
5 Food was rationed to overcome shortages.
6 The opening hours for the sale of alcohol were shortened. The government ordered strong beer to be watered down to reduce drunkenness at work.
7 The national anthem, 'God Save the King', was to be played after performances in theatres.

Recruitment

In the early years of the war there was tremendous enthusiasm for the war. Millions of men volunteered to fight for their country. In Britain Lord Kitchener, the Secretary for War, asked for 100 000 volunteers. The response was staggering. By the first week of September 1914, nearly 200 000 men had joined up and by the end of the month the number had risen to 750 000. In 1916 compulsory military service was introduced and the size of 'Kitchener's Army' rose to two and a half million. The minimum age of enlistment was 19 but this was often ignored. This soldier's account of how he enlisted when he was only 16 was typical of many thousands of young boys:

> *The recruiting sergeant asked me my age and when I told him he said, 'You had better go out, come in again, and tell me different'. I came back, told him I was nineteen and I was in.*

At the battle of Loos (1915) the ages of the soldiers involved ranged from 14 to 61 years old. One battalion of 'Kitchener's Army' had only three trained officers – one was stone deaf, another had a badly broken leg and the third, the commanding officer, was a 63-year-old retired veteran of the Boer War (1900)!

Using the evidence: oh what a lovely war!

Historians try to discover why people in the past acted in particular ways. This is often difficult to achieve. Why?

1 People do not always record their motives.
2 Other things may influence people as much as their own feelings and attitudes.

So can we discover why men went to fight in the Great War?

Read source A. It is a secondary piece of evidence because it is an imaginary account. Then study the other sources, which are primary, before answering the questions.

A *Breakfast time was unbearable again. The talk was all about the war, just as it had been for months. Mother preached about what would happen to innocent people if the Germans weren't defeated. Father buried his nose in the newspaper and read endless extracts from the battle reports. He said another conscientious objector had been sent to prison.
I walked to work as usual. A military band marched along the street, playing stirring tunes and men were encouraged to follow on behind it – to the recruiting office! There are posters everywhere. No wonder my friend George joined up yesterday. Two days earlier a woman had given him a white feather – the new symbol of cowardice. I haven't joined up but the war seems to be all around me. Tomorrow I will go to the recruitment office. Tomorrow I become a soldier.*

B *One morning I left home to go to work: we were repairing roads at the time, but on the way I met a friend who was going to enlist. Instead of going on to work, I went back home, changed into my best clothes and went with him to the recruiting office.*
Quoted in A. Lloyd's book, *The War in the Trenches*, 1976

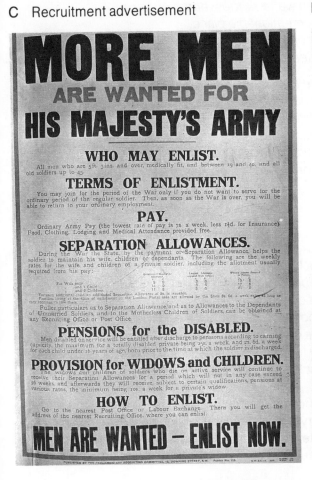

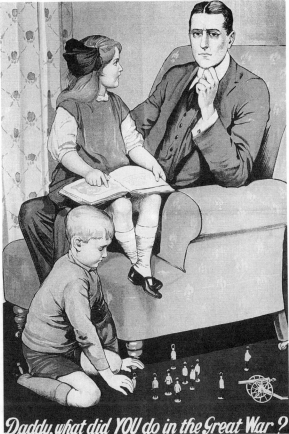

E A newspaper report about the battle of the Somme

July 3, 1916   THE DAILY MIRROR   Page 3

ADVANCE OF ALLIES IN THE WEST STILL CONTINUES

Capture of Fricourt by British with Substantial Progress—French Take Curlu.

HAUL OF PRISONERS NOW AMOUNTS TO 8,500

Germans Admit Front Line Trenches Were Taken—"Immovable Material Lost"—"Allies' Heavy Losses."

(BRITISH OFFICIAL.)

GENERAL HEADQUARTERS, Sunday, 5.5 p.m.

Substantial progress has been made in the vicinity of Fricourt, which was captured by our troops by 2 p.m. to-day.

Up to noon to-day some 800 more prisoners have been taken in the operations between the Ancre and the Somme, bringing the total up to 3,500, including those captured on other parts of the front last night.

(FRENCH OFFICIAL.)

PARIS, Sunday.—The following communiqué was issued this afternoon:—

To the north of the Somme fighting was furious during the night. The Germans launched violent counter-attacks against our new positions on the outskirts of Heudicourt.

Our curtain fire and our rifle fire inflicted serious losses on the enemy, who had to fall back in disorder, leaving 200 prisoners in our hands, of whom six were officers.

Pursuing our advantage on the right bank of the river, we gained possession after a sharp fight of the village of Curlu, which we occupied completely.

South of the Somme we have maintained all the positions captured by us yesterday, and have made some progress in the course of the night between Herbecourt and Assevillers.

According to further information to hand, the total figure of unwounded German prisoners captured by the French troops yesterday exceeds 5,000.

Between the Oise and the Aisne we captured a German patrol which tried to approach our lines near Bailly.—Reuter.

"PENETRATED OUR FIRST LINE TRENCHES."

(GERMAN OFFICIAL.)

The German official communiqué issued yesterday, says the Wireless Press, is as follows:—

The great English-French offensive "mass attack," which has been extensively prepared for during many months past, began yesterday over a front of twenty-five miles, after strong artillery and gas preparation lasting six days.

On both sides of the Somme, and likewise the Ancre Brook, from Gommecourt as far as the region of La Boiselle, the enemy obtained no advantages worthy of mention. He sustained, however, very heavy losses.

On the other hand, he was successful in penetrating at several points the first-line trenches of our division in the region abutting both banks of the Somme, and was able to advance.

This division had to be withdrawn from their heavily-shelled first-line trenches into the position arranged for, checking an advance from the first to the second lines.

The material in the first line, which was immovable and had been rendered useless as is customary in such cases, was lost.

In connection with these extensive operations there were many artillery actions and numerous minor attacks on the adjoining front, and also west and south-east of Tahure. They were everywhere unsuccessful.

FRENCH HOLD FAST TO | BRITISH MONITORS FIRE

Map showing Thiaumont Work.

"A VERY SATISFACTORY FIRST DAY."

Further Developments Can Be Awaited with Confidence.

ALLIES' LOSSES SLIGHT.

PARIS, Sunday.—A semi-official statement issued last night says:—

The chief fact of July 1 on the western front was the beginning of the Franco-British offensive.

By a very extended bombardment, the enemy was kept in ignorance as to the possible field of attack, and consequently had to divide his reserve effectives and to disperse his artillery.

The attack began at half-past seven in the morning and was preceded for half an hour by an artillery preparation the violence of which has never yet been equalled.

At nine o'clock the advanced defences of the German lines had fallen into our power.

The enemy's retreat made us masters of the villages of Montauban and Mametz, in the English zone, Becquincourt, Bussu and Fay, in the French zone.

According to the first information, our losses are few, as the result of the efficacy of our pre-

THE GREAT SQUEEZE.

BRITISH—North of Somme: We break into German forward defences on front of sixteen miles. Serre, Montauban, La Boiselle taken; Fricourt surrounded; German labyrinth of trenches on seven-mile front to depth of 1,000 yards captured. Prisoners : 2,000.

FRENCH—South of Somme: Dompierres, Becquincourt, Bussu, Fay and Curlu taken. Prisoners : 5,000.

ITALIAN—Italians still rolling back the Austrians to the Trentino.

RUSSIAN—Russians still moving ahead in Galicia and Bukowina. Total haul of prisoners : 217,000.

DESPERATE BLOWS AT RUSSIANS REPULSED.

Retreating Germans Fired On by Own Artillery.

BALTIC SEA SCRAP.

(RUSSIAN OFFICIAL.)

PETROGRAD, Saturday (received yesterday).—The communiqué issued to-day says :—

Western Front.—In the region between the Stokhod and the Styr the enemy is maintaining violent artillery fire.

Desperate fighting has begun in the village of Zaturtsy, where, in spite of a bombardment by the enemy of extreme violence, our troops have already repulsed nine successive attacks with heavy losses on the enemy.

In our sector of this region the Germans who were falling back were fired upon by their own batteries and forced to return to the attack.

The whole ground in this district is covered with enemy corpses.

Yesterday afternoon the enemy artillery produced gusts of fire in the region of Koptiche, Ghelenovka and Zabary, south-west of Sokul.

An energetic infantry attack then followed, but was repulsed.

MASSED ASSAULT STOPPED.

South-east of Kisseline our fire stopped an offensive by massed formations of the enemy in the village of Semerinka, and in the same region near the village of Zublino there was a warm engagement.

South of the village of Zaturtsy, near the village of Koscheff, we stopped an Austrian offensive by a counter-offensive.

We repulsed hostile attempts to cross the river Schara south-west of Lipsk, south of Baranowitchi.

Our left wing continues to throw the enemy back on the front south of the Dniester and has occupied several points north of Kolomea.

South-west of that town our troops, after hot fighting, repulsed the enemy towards the heights near the village of Brezovo.

We have already taken part of these heights.

North-west of Kimpolung the enemy, who endeavoured to take the offensive, was thrown back to the west.

217,000 PRISONERS NOW.

In this region our troops are pressing closely upon the enemy and have taken some strongly organised mountain positions.

The total number of prisoners taken by General Letchitsky during June 23 and 29 is 300 officers and 14,576 men. Four guns and thirty-two machine guns were also taken.

The grand total of prisoners taken from June 4 to June 30 is 217,000, officers included.

In the Baltic yesterday a detachment of ...

F
You love us when we're heroes, home on leave,
Or wounded in a mentionable place.
You worship decorations; you believe
That chivalry redeems the war's disgrace.

You can't believe that troops retire
When hell's last horror breaks them and they run,
Trampling the terrible corpses – blind with blood.
O German mother dreaming by the fire,
While you are knitting socks to send your son
His face is trodden deeper in the mud.

Siegfried Sassoon, 1917

G A French propaganda poster

1 Does source **A** explain exactly why the soldier joined up? Explain your conclusions.
2 How many *possible* motives can you find in source **A**? Can you say which of these had *the most influence* on the soldier or were they all important? Explain.
3 Study each of the other sources carefully. Which of them could be used to throw light on the soldier's account? Match the sources to particular parts of source **A**, and explain your choice.
4 Which of the sources help to explain why people enlisted in the armed forces? Try to complete the table below by matching up the list of possible reasons and the sources (**A** to **G**). When you have done this, suggest other reasons and sources for the table.

Reasons for enlistment	Source(s)
1 Patriotic feelings for one's country.	?
2 Misleading impression of what the war was like.	?
3 ?	B
4 Comradeship.	?
5 ?	C
6 Anger against a brutal enemy.	?
7 Others?	?

Women at war

After the war the British Prime Minister, Lloyd George, paid a glowing tribute to women workers:

It would have been utterly impossible for us to have waged a successful war had it not been for the skill, enthusiasm and industry which the women of this country have thrown into the war.

Shells, Shells, Shells! A British munitions factory. From January to March 1916, only $4\frac{1}{2}$ million shells were produced. From October to December 21 million were produced

As the men went off to war the women took over their jobs. By 1918 there were 1.3 million more women at work than in 1914. To maintain the war effort and day-to-day life at home they did every conceivable job: munitions work, farming, nursing and plumbing – and some even became undertakers! In Scotland women built ships and in Paris they ran the trains. Over 60 per cent of workers in the British munitions industry were women.

Casualties

Death touched nearly every family. The signs of mourning could be seen all around. Long lists of casualties were published in the daily newspapers and families anxiously studied them for news of loved ones and acquaintances. More dreadful was the arrival of telegrams with their short, stunning messages. Telegrams were sent to the next of kin when a soldier was killed or went missing. The one below arrived at Christmas, 1915.

> *T. 223 Regret to inform you Lieut. R. A. Leighton, 7th Worcesters died of wounds December 23rd. Lord Kitchener sends his sympathy.*

The British government tried to disguise the full horrors and high casualty figures and by 1918 the casualty figures were no longer published.

The wounded who were shipped back to Britain were taken to London hospitals in secrecy, but news of their terrible injuries soon got out. By 1917 ordinary people wanted the war to stop although at

Women at war: heaving coke

the same time they knew that it must continue. Cartoons in the popular magazine *Punch* urged people to 'Stand up for King and country' at the beginning of the war; by 1917 the slogan had changed to a grim 'Carry on'.

In Britain and Germany there were very few civilian casualties. Even though German cruisers shelled the towns of Bridlington, West Hartlepool, Scarborough and Whitby in 1915, and there were air raids on London and the south-east later on, for most people the war seemed a comfortable distance away. In France, however, it was a different story. Lives were lost and property destroyed each hour of every day.

Shortages and strikes

A British poster attacking luxurious living. Most people economised throughout the war

Nothing brought the hardship of war home to people more than food shortages. In 1917 a journalist commented that 'a lack of bacon would depress Great Britain even more than the biggest casualty list'. The submarines and naval blockades of ports created serious shortages of all basic materials. In Wrexham a farm-wagon full of potatoes

> ... *was surrounded by hundreds of clamouring people, chiefly women, who scrambled on to the vehicle in their eagerness to buy. Several women fainted in the struggle and the police were sent for to restore order.*

People grew used to long queues for food. Some queues were 4 000 people strong! Milk, butter and margarine became very scarce, while sugar was virtually impossible to obtain.

In France shortages caused the cost of living to rise by over 80 per cent. Civilians shivered through the winter of 1916–17 without coal and restaurants were closed down. Germany suffered worst of all due to the Allied naval blockade. There were frequent strikes for more food and public parks were dug up and sown with crops. A soap shortage caused a huge increase in body lice.

In all the countries involved in the war great campaigns were launched to recycle waste products. Bones, for example, were used for a variety of vital products – soap for washing, glue for aircraft, glycerine for explosives and fertilisers for farming. Human hair was used to make belts for driving machinery.

New laws had to be passed. In Britain it became illegal to throw rice at weddings or to feed pigeons. Restaurants were allowed to use potatoes on only two days each week. Foxes were shot on a large scale to protect poultry.

As the war dragged on people became bitter and weary. Despite government warnings and public criticism workers went on strike for higher pay or in protest against the war. In 1917 France was hit by 689 different strikes. In 1918 German strikers were shot dead.

THE FINAL ACTS

This morning came to an end the cruellest and most terrible war that has ever scourged mankind ... thus ... came to an end all wars.
David Lloyd George, 11 November 1918

Exit Russia, enter America

1917 ended badly for the Allies. There was slaughter at Passchendaele and disappointment at Cambrai. Added to this, there was the growing weakness of several countries. One government official wrote anxiously:

Russia has collapsed as a state.... Italy is torn by conflicting sympathies and hopes and fears; France is very, very tired.

Russia's withdrawal from the war and peace treaty with the Germans at Brest Litovsk (3 March 1918) was a serious blow to the Allies. It allowed the Germans to switch their eastern front troops to the west, and gave Germany the grain areas of western Russia, more industry and nearly all the Russian coal mines.

And yet, by the end of the year, the Allies had won the war! What happened, therefore, to change their fortunes? In the first place, Germany's campaign of unrestricted submarine warfare had failed. Secondly, the Allied naval blockade of German ports had brought the country to a state of virtual collapse. Starvation and disease, disillusionment and strikes were now the main features of daily life in Germany. Later in the year military defeats led to food riots and in October there was a naval mutiny at Kiel. An outbreak of a vicious virus, known as 'Spanish influenza', put the finishing touches to German morale and resistance. More than 1700 people died of the virus in Berlin on one day alone. At the fighting front Ludendorff reported that the soldiers jeered at the new German recruits for coming and prolonging the war.

Perhaps the most important reason for the turnaround in the war was the entry of America into the fighting. Anti-German feeling had grown in America, mainly because of the sinking of the *Lusitania* in 1915, and the discovery in 1917 that the Germans were secretly encouraging Mexico to invade the United States. Almost limitless money, equipment and troops were poured in by America to break the deadlock. By the end of 1917 over one million fresh troops had already arrived in France. Each month after this 225000 more American soldiers arrived to attack the exhausted and demoralised German army.

Ludendorff's gamble

For Germany, 1918 was to be a race against time. Ludendorff decided to launch one massive last offensive against the Allies before the Americans arrived. If the plan succeeded he would win the war. If it failed, Germany would be overpowered by the Americans.

The offensive began in March 1918 and was at first brilliantly successful. The Germans advanced 64 kilometres and broke through the gap between British and French troops. The Germans forced both armies into retreat. By July the Germans were closer to Paris than they had been in 1914. For a moment it looked as though Ludendorff's gamble had succeeded. A huge salient, 128 kilometres wide, had been created in the Allied territory. The Germans stood poised for the final victory.

On 18 July 1918, however, General Ferdinand Foch, the new overall commander of the Allied armies, ordered a counter-attack. The assault was spearheaded by thousands of tanks. At Amiens alone more than 600 tanks were used. They smashed enemy artillery and penetrated through enemy lines, going deep into German territory. The exhausted German troops had run out of supplies and offered little resistance.

On 26 September 1918 Foch ordered an all-out attack on the German lines. It met with almost total success. The great German war machine was now in its death throes. On 9 November the Kaiser fled to Holland and abdicated his throne. He was never to return to Germany. Ludendorff, by now a broken man, almost deranged, fled to Sweden in disguise. On 11 November, at 11 o'clock in the morning, an armistice was signed in Foch's railway headquarters. The Great War was over.

The peace settlement

In Paris the representatives of 28 victorious nations met to decide what should happen to the losers of the Great War – Germany, Austro-Hungary, Bulgaria and the Ottoman Empire. The fate of Europe was discussed at various palaces around Paris.

In practice the peace settlement was dominated by three men: David Lloyd George (Prime Minister of Britain), Woodrow Wilson (President of the United States) and Georges Clemenceau (Premier of France). All three men wanted to avoid a future war. Each was worried that an unstable Europe might be influenced by Communist ideas. Each accepted to different degrees that Germany should be punished. On many other points, however, the peacemakers disagreed.

In the end the settlement was a compromise. Very few people were completely happy with it. Some felt angry and bitter.

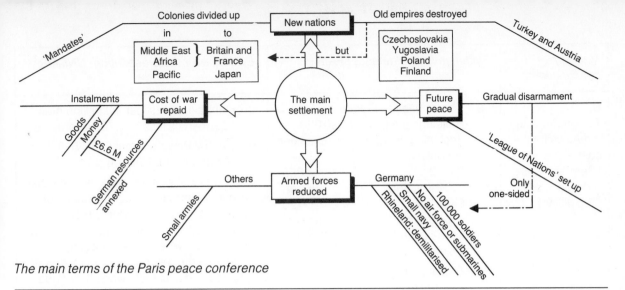

The main terms of the Paris peace conference

Using the evidence: the peacemakers?

A specific treaty was signed with Germany at the Palace of Versailles. This treaty has been criticised for being unfair. Here is what one man said ten years later:

> *It was a piece of vengeance. It reeked with injustice. . . . It sowed a thousand seeds from which new wars might spring . . . the ideals for which millions of men had fought and died – liberty, fair play, a war to end war, justice – were mocked and outraged, not by men of evil, but by good men, not by foul design, but by loyalty to national interests.*
>
> Quoted in J. Hamer's book, *The Twentieth Century*, 1980

On the other hand the peacemakers had a very difficult task.

   Use the evidence to answer the questions below, then put the settlement on trial – fair or unfair!

Main aim of peacemakers	Evidence for the defence: FAIR	Evidence for the prosecution: UNFAIR
A To be fair and moral.	1 A graph showing Russia's losses to Germany after the treaty of Brest Litovsk. Industry 54%, Coal mines 89%, Population 25%, Wheat 30%. Russia also forced to pay 6 billion marks. 2 Many different views had to be taken into account. Not everybody could be satisfied.	a 'Germany accepts the responsibility . . . for causing all the loss and damage . . . as a consequence of the war imposed . . . by the aggression of Germany and her Allies.' Clause 231 of the treaty b The main decisions of the peacemakers were taken in secret. Russia and Germany and its allies were not even allowed to take part in the conference.

Main aim of peacemakers	Evidence for the defence: FAIR	Evidence for the prosecution: UNFAIR
B To compensate the Allies for the cost of the war. (Germany was ordered to pay £6.6 billion).	3 *The damage to France* Buildings destroyed: 290 000 (including factories, churches and schools) Forest destruction 4 856 sq. km Farmland destruction 20 720 sq. km Loss of human lives 1 350 000 4 Total expenditure by Allies: £27 909 million. 5 The Allied casualties in the war.	c Central Powers lost 3.2 million men (Germany's loss = 1.75 million). d Central Powers spent £13 476 million (Germany = £8 394 m). e 'It was just as if one took the view that every German worker on starvation wages, every little seamstress, or university student, ten or twelve years old when the war began, shares the responsibility of those war lords and militarists who challenged the world in 1914. . . .' Sir Philip Gibbs, 1929
C To allow small states to decide their own affairs.	6 Disputed territories were to be allowed to vote to decide which nation they would belong to ('plebiscites'). 7 Germany had its colonies taken away. 8 The political map of Europe was virtually 're-drawn' to give independence to small nations and racial groups.	f Alsace and Lorraine were not allowed a plebiscite. g Most German and Turkish colonies were taken over by Britain, France and Japan. h (i) Seven million Germans now found themselves living in Poland, Alsace, Lorraine and Czechoslovakia. (ii) Several different races were forced to live together in countries such as Yugoslavia and Czechoslovakia.

Europe after Versailles

Key
1 FINLAND
2 ESTONIA
3 LATVIA
4 LITHUANIA
5 EAST PRUSSIA
6 NETHERLANDS
7 BELGIUM
8 CZECHOSLOVAKIA
9 SWITZERLAND
10 AUSTRIA
11 HUNGARY
12 BESSARABIA
13 BULGARIA
14 ALBANIA
15 GREECE

Lost by Germany   Lost by Russia

Main aim of peacemakers	Evidence for the defence: FAIR	Evidence for the prosecution: UNFAIR
D To prevent future wars and encourage democracy.	9 The League of Nations was set up to provide a forum for peaceful negotiation instead of war – 'collective security'. However, it was given no army to enforce its decisions. 10 Disarmament was recommended and partly achieved: 11 Democracies were encouraged in Europe.	i The League refused entry to Russia and Germany. All countries had one vote, regardless of size, wealth or power. For example: New Zealand 1.3 million population China 500 million population j

Disarmament table (within cell 10):

	Army	Navy and Air force
Germany	100 000 only	No submarines
Austria	30 000 only	No air force Small navy

Map (j): Trouble spots after 1918
0 300 km
Key
Countries under dictatorship as a result of post-war tensions
○ Trouble spots
Ⓛ Lost territory
Ⓑ Border conflict
Ⓝ National minority
Ⓔ Economic problem

The judgement

Answer the following questions and then use your answers as a guideline for your trial of the settlement and the peacemakers. Also use the rest of the book and your own knowledge and skills to help you. A good historian/lawyer must consider both sides of the argument and must weigh up the evidence carefully before making a judgement.

1 a) Was Germany's treatment of Russia harsh (A:1)?
  b) Can we assume that Germany would have done the same kind of thing to the other Allies if she had won the war?
  c) Are these terms (A:1) any worse than those imposed on Germany by the Allies (e.g. £6.6 billion reparations)?

2 Why do you think that many people after 1919 thought that Clause 231 (A:a) was untruthful? (See chapter 2.) Why were the peacemakers determined to blame Germany?

3 Consider D:i. How realistic were these terms?

4 Study D:j carefully and compare it to other maps in the book.
  a) Why were there 'trouble spots' in these places?
  b) Does the map prove that the peace settlement failed?

5 Consider the evidence for and against Aim C. Then decide how far each of the following words could be used to describe the terms of the settlement (C:6–8 and C:f–g).
  (i) contradictory   (ii) hypocritical   (iii) realistic

6 Study the evidence under Aim B.
  a) Why were the French determined to 'make Germany pay'?
  b) Who lost most during the war?
  c) In 1919 the German economy was exhausted. Any amount of reparations would take decades to pay. Is B:e written with the benefit of hindsight? Is it, therefore, valid evidence? Explain your answer.

INDEX

Numerals in **bold** denote illustrations

aircraft, 25, 43, 44–5, **44**
alliances, 9, 10–11
Allies, the, 14, 20, 35, 38, 41, 52, 59, 60, 62–3
arms race, 12
Arras, 25, 42

Balkan League and wars, 16
Balkan states, 15–16, **17**
barbed wire, 29
Black Hand, 5,6
Bosnia, 9, 16
Brest Litovsk, 37, 59, 61
British Expeditionary Force, 19
Brusilov's offensive, 36

casualties, 21, **29**, 30, 37, 38, 39, **39**, 40, 45, 57–8, **62**
causes of the war, 8–18
Central Powers, **17**, 35, 38, 52
civilian involvement, 52, 56–7, 62

'*Dreadnoughts*', 12, 46
dug-outs, 25, **29**, **32**

eastern front, 21, 24, 35, 36–7
effects of war, 61–3
empires and colonialism, 5, 8–9, 16
Entente Cordiale, 10

Falkenhayn, Erich von, 21, 38, 39
Franz Ferdinand, 5, 6, **7**, 8
French, Sir John, 19, 20, 35

Gallipoli, 52

gas, 35, **36**

Haig, Douglas, 35, 38, 39, 41
'Hindenberg Line', **40**, 41
Hindenberg, Paul von, 22, 24

Italy, 35, 52

Joffre, General, 20, 38
Jutland, 48–50

Kiel Canal, 12, **50**
kit and equipment, 28
Kitchener, Lord, 53, 54

League of Nations, 61, 63
Lemberg, 24
Lloyd George, David, 53, 56, 59, 60
Loos, 27, 28, 35, 54
Ludendorff, Erich, 22, 24, 39, 41, 59, 60
Lusitania, 47, 59

machine guns, 28
Marne, 20, 25
mining, 46
Moltke, Helmuth von, 20, 21
Mons, 19
Moroccan incidents, 9

nationalism, 15
navies, 12, 46–8
Nivelle, Robert, 42

offensives, 18–21, 24, 35, 36, 38, 41, 42, 60
Old Contemptibles, 19

Paris Peace Conference, 60–3

Passchendaele, 27, 42, 59
Pétain, Henri Philippe, 38
popular attitudes, 13
Princip, Gavrilo, 6, 7, 8
propaganda, 13, **14**, 37, 55, **56**

railways, 9, 13, 14, 21
recruitment 53–6, **55**
Rennenkampf, 22

Samsonov, Alexander, 21–2, 24
Sarajevo, 5, 16–17
Schlieffen Plan, 13–14, 19
Serbia, 5, 16, 21, 24
shortages and strikes, 58
Somme, 25, **26**, 27, 39–41, 55

tanks, **25**, 39, 42, 60
Tannenberg, 21–4
technology and warfare, 25, 45, 46–7
trench warfare, 25, 26, **27**, 28
daily life, 30–4, **32**
diseases, 30
'no man's land', 26, 29

U-boats, 41, 47, 51
USA, 59

Verdun, 28, 38

western front, **7**, 24, 26, 28, 37, 38, 52
Wilhelm II, 8, **14**, 15, 19
women at war, 56–7, **57**

Ypres, 20–1, 35, 42

Zeppelins, 45